The Wisdom of Storytelling in an Information Age

A Collection of Talks

Amy E. Spaulding

The Scarecrow Press, Inc.
Lanham, Maryland • Toronto • Oxford
2004

SCARECROW PRESS, INC.

Published in the United States of America
by Scarecrow Press, Inc.
A wholly owned subsidiary of
The Rowman & Littlefield Publishing Group, Inc.
4501 Forbes Boulevard, Suite 200, Lanham, Maryland 20706
www.scarecrowpress.com

PO Box 317
Oxford
OX2 9RU, UK

British Library Cataloguing in Publication Information Available

Library of Congress Cataloging-in-Publication Data

Spaulding, Amy E., 1944–
  The wisdom of storytelling in an information age : a collection of talks
/ Amy E. Spaulding.
    p. cm.
  Includes bibliographical references (p.   ).
  ISBN 0-8108-5044-3 (pbk. : alk. paper)
  1. Public speaking. 2. Storytelling. 3. Narration (Rhetoric) I. Title.
PN4193.I5S57 2004
808.5'1—dc22
                                            2004006091

♾™ The paper used in this publication meets the minimum requirements of
American National Standard for Information Sciences—Permanence of
Paper for Printed Library Materials, ANSI/NISO Z39.48-1992.
Manufactured in the United States of America.

This book is dedicated to the storyteller in each of us.

Many thanks to all those
who provided support for this book.

Contents

Contents

Foreword

In the beginning was the word. Long before humankind began to write down its thoughts and stories millennia ago, the world was the basis of the stories that the earliest people told themselves, huddled together in a hostile unpopulated world of hunting, gathering, caves, planes, light, and darkness. In that world, all that humans knew was contained in the places in which they lived, the lives that they lived, and the stories that transcended time, space, and reality. Perhaps there were stories before there was human-created and controlled fire and those stories were all that kept the families and small bands of early humans together and comforted in the deep darkness. The story was the binding force in the earliest human societies; the story was their religion, their science, their entertainment, their history, their mirror, and their telescope through which they peered into the past and the future. The storyteller was a magus, a shaman, a priest, and repository of wisdom.

Just as the earliest people were in thrall to the story, so are we moderns in our earliest years. One of the foundations of a happy childhood lies in that memory of being told a story in the semi-darkness by a parent or other adult. Later, we remember listening to a children's librarian or a teacher reading to us and we remember re-creating that earliest experience of the story by reading a book in a dimly lit bedroom or, even better, under the covers with a flashlight. The popularity of audio books on tape and CD is attributed to our car-ridden society and attempts to alleviate the agony of long commutes, but surely it has even more to do with that fundamental human urge to listen to the shaman, the sage, the wise woman, the storyteller and, in doing so, to know the comfort and fascination of the story. Pre-historic people huddled in a cave, drowsy children demanding a well known story, and a commuter on the San Diego Freeway in the rush hours are all linked by the atavistic experience of the enduring story.

Amy Spaulding has done us all a great service in this fascinating collection of essays, all based, most fittingly, on those stories we call papers—spoken communications from the wise to the open minded. The essays are even more valuable in this "age of information," in which we humans are constantly tempted to worship the false gods of technology and consider ourselves better than our ancestors because we are skilled in the lightning fast transmission of snippets of information. This *hubris* is misplaced because it ignores the value of knowledge and wisdom, exalts the value of data and information, and down values the human heart and the human imagination. What counts are stories, not the means by which those stories are conveyed. The important things are imagination and creativity, not appliances. Would Dickens or Shakespeare have been "better" if they had a word processor (the very term is like a knell) rather than a steel or quill pen? Is a wise woman in the firelight "worse" than a rubbishy writer with an I-Mac? The questions are absurd because, deep in our hearts, we know that stories are more powerful than machines, that myths and dreams still govern the human condition, and that words, ideals, and stories dominate our waking and sleeping hours. That last is as true today as it was in the dawn of humankind.

Dr. Spaulding covers every aspect of this central topic and, in reading this valuable book, the reader comes to understand the continuity and value of the story and storytelling to modern humans of all ages and the vital importance of seeing beyond the flash and glitter of modern technology to the golden thread of the story—the golden thread that defines our humanity.

Michael Gorman
California State University, Fresno

Michael Gorman is dean of Library Services at the Henry Madden Library at California State University, Fresno. He has taught at library schools in his native Great Britain and in the United States, most recently at the University of California, Los Angeles. A prolific author, Gorman was the first editor of the *Anglo-American Cataloging Rules, Second Edition* and author of two award-winning books, *Future Libraries: Dreams, Madness and Reality* and *Our Enduring Values*. His newest book is *The Enduring Library: Technology, Tradition and the Quest for Balance*.

Chapter 1

Introduction:
What Is the Wisdom in Storytelling?

This chapter and the last one were written for the book rather than presented, so you, as reader, are the only audience. The format is no different, however, for these chapters contain stories, and your own silently heard voice must provide the only "talk"

> *Time comes into it.*
> *Say it. Say it.*

> *The universe is made of stories,*
> *Not of atoms.*

Muriel Rukeyser[1]

Storytelling is valuable for many different reasons. It is an organic art and, as more and more of life becomes technologized, it grows in importance as an antidote to impersonality. Also, as the world of scholarship gets closer to the scientific equivalent of how many angels are dancing on the head of a pin, it is good to remember the wisdom in looking at the forest as well as the trees, and story is good for maintaining broader perspectives. The talks in this book were all meant to remind their listeners of why it is important and were written in the passionate personal voice of story, occasionally even in the form of narrative. Because the audiences were quite different, the subject is approached from a variety of directions. Some audiences were academic, some professional, and some simply interested in the subject, perhaps as parents or teachers.

As a book it is meant for dipping into, like a group of short stories, rather than for reading cover to cover like a novel. It should be read as shared thoughts rather than as conference papers presenting research to prove theories; it is, however, scholarly in the sense that there are many references to experts in a variety of fields, so that readers can follow up ideas and come to their own conclusions. The intent is not to convert everyone into platform storytellers but to start readers thinking about how story is interwoven into our lives and start them noticing how story is being coopted by some groups who see its power without respecting or understanding its nature.

People often ask how I happened to become interested in storytelling. The short answer is simple. My family told stories. Perhaps I was doomed by genetics or, perhaps, it was the environment—but I come by being both a storyteller and an academic honestly. My grandfather was a minister, my father an English professor, and my mother a psychiatrist. Thus, I got parables, literature and life stories. In college I majored in anthropology and minored in theater. My first career, that of children's librarian, required storytelling.

My father used to tell great bedtime stories—his own as well as folk tales—and although I don't remember many tales, I do remember the sense of wholeness that the experience brought. My mother often used stories to convince us of ideas. One of them provides a good point to begin from because it shows the power of storytelling in everyday life.

I had told her how startled I was by the way my brazen patter as auctioneer for a charity event had convinced people to spend a lot of money. She responded with an anecdote about our own family and how she frightened herself by spinning a convincing story.

My big brother got a paper route when he was about eleven. After working all fall, he went shopping for Christmas presents with his huge fortune. (This was long enough ago that his five dollar bill had considerable buying power.) He had done careful window shopping before finally selecting purchases at the dime store; glass dishes for his mother, a pen for his father, paper dolls for his little sister, and bath powder for both grandmothers. Having done the addition in his head, he knew that he had all the money he needed, even for tax, and began the actual buying at the counter with the dishes. He watched as the salesgirl wrapped and bagged all eight little glass bowls, then reached into his pocket for the five dollar bill. It was GONE. All of his jacket, shirt, and pants pockets were checked, along with the floors by all the counters at which he had stopped. It did no good. Magic did not happen. The money was GONE. The girl was nice about it, even though the store was busy and she did not have time to waste, but it was hu-miliating, nonetheless. All that work, all that saving, and nothing to show for it. Worst of all was the thought of spending another Christmas in the role of boy rather than as a noble, generous, wage-earning young man.

By the time he got home, he was close to tears and could hardly bear to tell his mother what had happened. Money was fairly tight, so there was no way she could just replace it. Gone was gone. Still, she could try to comfort him, so she stopped her cookie baking and be-gan to talk. As she praised him for his generous plans and tried to reconcile him to the reality, she began to wonder aloud what had happened to the money.

It could be under a counter at the store, or it could have been taken by someone dishonest, but it might . . . just might . . . have been simply lost and then found by someone who really needed it—maybe even another boy, from a really poor family with no money at all for Christmas.

It was amazing how much that five dollars could accomplish. It bought a turkey, potatoes, green beans, pumpkin for pie, and cranberries. Oh, yes, there were enough cranberries left to string with popcorn to decorate the tree that was bought for change from a man who sold it cheaply because he had only one tree left and wanted to go home. I am not sure whether it took care of a sick grandmother, or bought fuel for the furnace, or whether Tiny Tim was there, but that money certainly managed to buy a very Merry Christmas for that needy family.

Santa Claus was introduced to take care of presents, since little sister Amy was in the kitchen, listening too. At any rate, my brother was significantly cheered up by the story; even if it was only a "maybe" it was a good story with a happy ending.

That is important, but what is even more relevant for this book is the epilogue. Just as she saw her son's face and felt pleased with herself, she was badly shaken by that little sister's voice, first giving a deep sigh and then piping up: "Gee, I wish I had lost five dollars."

Be warned: my mother was right and the power of story is not to be taken lightly—nor the fact that story is a collaborative effort. Many times a listener will thank (or blame) the storyteller for a tale that supports an idea that the teller never saw in it. The listener's role is no less important than the storyteller's in the creation of any story, and the combination does not always produce the expected conclusion. An early mystery writer understood this saying: "It is a law of the story-teller's art that he does not tell a story. It is the listener who tells it. The story-teller does but provide him with the stimuli"[2]

In the case of my mother's story, my admiration of my big brother and my six-year-old's logic combined to make me want to emulate him. The storyteller's adult logic found my conclusion ludicrous, but her intention was irrelevant; that's what I got out of it. Who knows, perhaps her story is why I have yet to become rich. Or, perhaps, it is why I became a storyteller. I don't know. My brother remembers the incident, but all I remember is her telling me the story about her story.

The point is that storytelling is a living process, not a predictable, controllable one. There is an element of mystery to it. That is how it differs from the transfer of information, and what makes it valuable and powerful in its own way. Both are needed, but only very recently has the awareness that too much information can create problems become a concern, and attention has come back to flexible story, which was the normal way of sharing ideas for millennia before modern attempts to control it with technology began with Gutenberg's moveable type.

Concern about the impact of technology (primarily the media and computers) is a sub-theme through these lectures. Many theorists have discussed the impact in terms of society, but not many have related it to story. To prevent readers assuming that I am a Luddite, I would like to state that I first became involved with computers in the 1970s, have taught on-line searching, and have worked with technology support for individuals with impairments. The advantages and abilities of information technology are great; we just need to think through its various impacts and choose where to use such tools wisely. There is a funny modern legend, perhaps true, that NASA spent millions designing a pen to write in zero gravity, while the Russians used a pencil. High-tech is not always the best choice, and that is as true with ideas as with objects.

We must be responsible to ourselves and to the future, both by assessing the impact of all this attention to information and its technology on us as human beings as well as consumers, and by trying to maintain what is essential from more traditional forms. I believe that person to person storytelling is one of those essential forms, not just for the content of the tales, but for the connection between the individuals involved, whether there is a single listener or a large audience.

Story is not generally recognized outside of what is identified as narrative, but it is everywhere. Like the fish that did not know it was in water, in the parable Marshall McLuhan used to warn us about the impact of the media surrounding us, we often don't realize the extent to which we live in story or recognize its influence. Each of us is largely a product of his or her own stories—the ones lived, the ones believed, the ones heard, read, and told. These include not only those of self, family, and groups we identify with, and those created by narrative artists we admire, but also an overwhelming number produced by commercial "talent" for consumption as entertainment, public relations, propaganda, or commercial advertising. These are not consciously taken in as story, but they are. These are all too often meant to convince us for the betterment of the tellers' own pockets and purposes, rather than the betterment of humankind. Many of theses are really good stories, but many others are not, and all are affecting our view of the world, consciously or unconsciously.

Story is a form of information, and information is a form of realistic story. As information is being commodified, what is happening to story? Is story just one more product to be consumed? If who we are is largely composed of stories, is it dangerous for us to become just passive consumers, choosing from what is offered commercially? Is it important to keep live stories and storytelling as well as captured information?

I believe it is, and hope you can share my respect and enthusiasm for story and that you will find some of the questions posed valuable springboards for your own ideas.

One final note. Back in the 1936 Walter Benjamin warned that: "The art of storytelling is reaching its end because the epic side of truth, wisdom, is dying out."[3] This dark prediction will, I hope, prove wrong on both counts. The title of this book, *The Wisdom of Storytelling*, is meant to imply both that it is wise to tell stories and that stories will remain a source of wisdom as long as humankind exists.

Notes

1. Muriel Rukeyser, "The Speed of Darkness" verse 9, in *The Speed of Darkness* (New York: Random House, 1968). It was first read at M.I.T. [I met her a few years later and actually happened to tell her stories—on a bus on the way to an anti-war rally in Washington, D.C., organized by my landlord who was her friend.]

2. Melville Davisson Post, "The Doomdorf Mystery" (1914) in *The Oxford Book of American Detective Stories*. Edited by Tony Hillerman and Rosemary Herbert (New York: Oxford University Press, 1996), 88.

3. Walter Benjamin, "The Storyteller," section 4 in *Illuminations*. Edited with introduction by Hannah Arendt, translated by Harry Zohn (New York: Harcourt Brace & World, 1936 [1968]).

Chapter 2

The Importance of Story and Narrative Thinking

Introduction to the Talk

This was originally delivered at the Bank Street College of Education Library, New York, New York, September 25, 2002.

The first time I taught storytelling in a concentrated format, one student dubbed it "Storytelling Boot Camp" and the name stuck. That student became a friend and when she heard of the plan to turn this series of talks into a book, she invited me to come speak at the Bank Street College of Education.

It was good to be reminded of the way that storytelling is transmitted through time from one person to another and to feel that connection and be proud to be a part of it. The sense of the importance of that art and tradition to all people, regardless of their technological sophistication, was the motivation behind this talk.

The Importance of Story and
Narrative Thinking

The endless cycle of idea and action,
Endless invention, endless experiment,
Brings knowledge of motion, but not stillness.

. . . Where is the wisdom we have lost in knowledge?
Where is the knowledge we have lost in information?
T.S. Eliot[1]

We are finally coming to understand the crucial importance of imagination, not just from "entertainment" but also to maintain our mental health and to thrive as human beings. Again and again it becomes clear that one's perspective on events colors the perception of "what really happened." After a lifetime as a librarian and professor, dealing professionally with both information and story, I have come to believe that story is the more important of the two. Information is about the rational control of facts, useful harnessing of the raw material of data; story is about understanding and making meaning of those facts, and about giving them direction.

The fact that it was a poet who spoke about the differences between knowledge and wisdom introduces another factor. Information and knowledge today are managed from a binary, yes-no base. That fact has colored our concept of what information is.[2] If it does not fit within a system, it is devalued for not being "useful."

Wisdom requires an ability to think original thoughts. The closest we seem to come in the information world is the cliché "think outside the box." Literary, narrative, oral thinking is different; it combines logic with imagination rather than stopping at rational ratiocination.

Eliot's words catch this dilemma of our age. They also set out the reason behind this discussion. Information is a valuable commodity, but wisdom is invaluable; the two are not the same, and we are losing awareness of wisdom as the goal. My childhood, spent as a faculty brat watching my parents' extremely smart friends, taught me early that intelligence and common sense were not the same thing and did not necessarily appear in equal quantities within the same person. Likewise, although learning and wisdom often came together—having been inspired by sincere respect for truth—education could also produce smug arrogance or tunnel vision.

This mention of arrogance is also an indirect reminder of some corollary issues. Wisdom includes both humility and humor, which makes sense, since both require not taking oneself too seriously. Wisdom also requires the ability to shift perspective and focus quickly, so as to see many sides of the same issue.

Not all of life's questions can be answered with "yes" or "no," or even with a selection from multiple choice: often there are only shades of gray offered, though better answers may lie somewhere in the colors of the rainbow. Wisdom requires imaginative creativity on the one hand and judgment on the other. It requires the ability to discriminate between answers which are not right or wrong but have good and bad elements intermixed. The consequences must be imagined and thought through like chess moves.

This kind of creative thinking is fostered by narrative, which encourages story-listeners to consider several of the very different possible outcomes that might proceed from particular circumstances. Narrative develops sequential thinking and promotes the idea that someone can choose how to react to circumstances—and that different responses produce different outcomes that are worth thinking about beforehand—either as goals worth being pursued or as fates best avoided.

This concern for story might seem strange in a culture inundated by television, but it is relevant for a number of reasons. Part of it is that television shows the stories being acted out and watching doesn't require the imagination to work in the way it does when the tale is told in words alone. That is not the only reason, though. First, television is a medium that suggests reality. Just as photography and painting serve different functions, television does well at representing the realistic tenses, such as "is" or "will be" but less well at presenting the subjective tenses of "could be" and "may be" than the told story. This makes television effective for some kinds of imaginative fiction, such as chilling sci-fi with special effects, but generally better at semi-realistic stories 'than fantasy or myth, which depends on metaphor.[3] It is easier to identify with television characters as real people than as archetypical symbols to feed the sub-conscious.[4] Because of this characteristic of the medium, sitcoms and soap operas work very well; one knows the characters and their actions are those of everyday life—exaggerated to be sure, but still familiar.[5]

This propensity toward the realistic has meant that, unlike formal drama, which follows the conventions of written literature, television mimics everyday speech and, along with it, everyday values and opinions rather than heroic language and considered views. It is better at representing action than at presenting ideas. Television can provide fine entertainment and news or documentary coverage, but it does not inculcate narrative thinking.

Information and logic are useful, but dry. To the technocrats, for whom effectiveness is the highest priority, that is good enough. But from a creative or humanities perspective, the messy, organic nature of story makes it valuable. It can bend to the winds of changing circumstances. More than that, it has the beauty and warmth of living things. Humans are living beings, not just reasoning machines, and they respond to story in a more open and complete way than they do to recitation of facts. If you will forgive another analogy, it is like the difference between exercising in a techno-gym with weights machines and bicycle machines, as opposed to dancing at a wedding. Both are exercise, but one is imposing action on the body "for its own good" in disconnected "parallel play," and the other has the joy of connecting body and spirit together with others in pleasurable, social activity.

Before continuing with the serious concerns related to the need for story, it seems important to pause for a moment and underline the thought that storytelling engenders joy. Enthusiasm is a natural part of the form. Listening to stories—funny fables, touching romances, scary ghost tales, heroic sagas, inspirational myths—all of these produce delight in their hearers, and also bring joy to the teller. Stories are like gifts that enrich both giver and recipient.

There are those who say that story is what makes us humans, and we certainly seem to respond to narrative. Some people find storytelling not to their taste,[6] just as some find eating simply a matter of refueling and otherwise a waste of time, but for most of us story is a joy, and that makes it valuable for communication and as an art that enriches culture. We would leave society far poorer and weaker if we were to allow it to die out in our generation.

We are now overwhelmed with information overload, in an information-inflated environment. Data are being recorded, not because they have value, but because they can be collected. Information is recognized as powerful, but it is being used for inappropriate purposes that have been thought up but not thought though. The need to imagine impact and consider the philosophical aspects of these issues is crucial and is made more difficult because we have no equivalent in history to give us the wisdom of experience.[7] We have no relevant stories from which to work. The rational world of information is recognizing this lack and has tried to adapt story to its needs. For example, many companies have used such devices as scenario building to better predict the probable outcomes of ways that circumstances could play out.

The truth is that our stories underlie everything, even what is accepted as "fact." The debate over the theory of evolution in light of the "fact" of Genesis is but one example. We may agree on the Fahrenheit and Centigrade measurement of a day, but whether it is "too cold" or "too hot" is a matter of personal experience, which is based on differences in physical makeup and the stories we tell ourselves about what is an appropriate temperature. What brings this analogy to mind is experience with an Englishman who truly believed that central heating had ruined people's health and was the cause of most colds. That story seemed ludicrous to my shivering North American sensibilities.

Storytelling lies at a place that is very important in today's world—the border between rationality and art. It is about the creative imagination of metaphor and the ability to see things in layers of context. It even promotes "wisdom" and "integrity," which are still valuable, whether or not they are in fashion. Storytelling should not be about providing cute morals of the "and so we see that . . . " variety, but about cultivating the listener's ability to make meaning, for it is from this kind of meaning that morality grows.[8] It is no accident that great religious figures used story and parable so often. They teach how to think in comparison rather than just to follow rigid rules.[9] Story teaches the listener how to assess the spirit of the law, not just the letter of the law.

For a variety of historical reasons, oral culture has been associated with childhood and naiveté. But that culture can be as sophisticated as any logic-based field of study, and rather richer and more subtle in the bargain. We have reached a time when we recognized that controlling language to minimize ambiguity in data comes at considerable cost in creative imagination and limitations to communicating thought. The value of metaphor and unfettered vocabulary is being reconsidered.

Story's strength comes from many aspects that lie deep within us, and it is easy to wax poetic about its mystic powers, but that is for debate in other venues.[10] This discussion is based on three basic principles: the development of imagination is crucial, story is essential for imagination, and story helps us connect as human beings.

First, developing imagination is necessary and important. This has not been fully recognized in the past century; neither has it been recognized that the development of imagination beyond personal daydreams of glory or love or revenge is not as automatic as walking. Imagination seems to need encouragement to grow strong and in healthy directions.

Second, story is essential for the development of imagination. Literally. It is in listening to stories that we first learn to envision and thus become free to imagine on our own. There is also a big impact of story-based imagination on reading. The wish to reclaim oral culture should not be seen as a wish to displace reading; far from it. It should enhance reading enjoyment and skill by supporting comprehension at the same time that reading lessons are working on decoding skills. Sadly, even adults could use remedial imagination classes, because society has become more and more dependent on pre-made images.

Third, story can help us reconnect with our human roots, as we continue "technologizing" ourselves and changing what is means to be a "human" being.[11] Through most of human history story was the way of passing information orally from person to person and generation to generation.[12] We are "hard-wired" to story, to use a computer-based metaphor. It behooves us, therefore, to look at how it works.

Is there really a crisis in developing imagination? My experience with both children and adults suggests that people are finding it harder and harder to use their imaginations. That is not an uncommon perception and will be discussed later. Whether or not one chooses to blame the technology and media-driven world, there does seem to be a disturbing shift, with, on the one hand, the increasing need for creative imagination and, on the other, people being less agile in creativity. The modern world perceived that need in terms of inventiveness, rather than artistic creativity, but with the post-modern world, views are changing.

One of the watersheds in this shift was the development of serious study on the different functions of the right and left brain. People began to think about the implications for both education and business. A teacher of management had this to say, more than twenty years ago:

> Creative thinking requires coordinating and using *both* sides of the brain. Flashes of insight and intuition are the result of right-brain thinking but analyzing these insights must be carried out in the left brain. . . . When the results of split-brain research are considered in light of our education, a frightening fact emerges. *We're developing only the left side of our brain while the right side is being suppressed and ignored . . .*

> It's been said that the electronic computer is the first extension of man's mind. For the first time in history, man has a tool capable of logical and abstract thinking. . . . The challenge to industry, education and society is to develop right-brain thinking that will enable us to work in harmonious partnership with the giant, electronic left-brains that we have created.[13]

More recently, Kieran Egan, an expert in children's imaginative development, has expressed concern that this kind of imaginative thinking has not been developed. He has this to say:

> . . . the development of rationality, in cultural history and in individual's education, might be better understood if it is seen to grow out of, and on, our "poetic natures," or our orality. What is important to note, however, is that this process is not well understood if seen simply as a displacement of a confused, ineffective form of thinking with a "natural," effective rationality. Rather we need to see more clearly the positive features of orality and try to ensure that they are not suppressed in the development of literate rationality.
>
> . . . children's imaginations are the most powerful and energetic learning tools. Our most influential learning theories have been formed from research programs that have very largely focused on a limited range of children's logical thinking skills. That research has largely neglected imagination, because imagination is, after all, difficult stuff to get any clear hold on. Consequently the dominant learning theories that have profoundly influenced education, helping to form the dominant model and principles mentioned above, have taken little account of imagination.[14]

Story has always been associated with imagination. The National Council of Teachers of English (NCTE) clearly believes that storytelling is needed again, and published this statement:

> Once upon a time, oral storytelling ruled. It was the medium through which people learned their history, settled their arguments, and came to make sense of the phenomena of their world. Then along came the written word with its mysterious symbols. Oral storytelling, like the simpleminded youngest brother in the olden tales, was foolishly cast aside . . .
>
> The simpleminded youngest brother in olden tales, while disregarded for a while, won the treasure in the end every time.[15]

Those concerned with teaching English might be expected to recognize the value of story, but many others also respect its place in our lives. Futurologist Rolf Jensen, in his *The Dream Society: How the Coming Shift from Information to Imagination will Transform Your Business,*[16] says:

> In the Information Society, our work has been driven by information technology; in the Dream Society, our work will be driven by stories and emotions, not just by data. . . . [17] Anyone seeking success in the market of the future will have to be a storyteller. The story is the heart of the matter.[18]

His definition of story is rather broader than the tales of oral tradition, of course. His idea includes the stories we use to define ourselves and what have been called "master narratives." He is thinking of underlying values statements that may be:

> . . . stories about the universe and mankind's place in it, or they may be little everyday stories about who we are and who the others are. These stories may be transmitted orally, in written form, through images, in plays or movies, or through the very products we choose to be surrounded by.[19]

A perspective on this, closer to the more traditional view of story, that of the individual wishing to survive emotionally intact, is offered by Gianni Rodari's *Grammar of Imagination*, which came out of his concern that *everyone* should develop the ability to think and to express creatively. "The purpose is not . . . to become artists, but . . . to avoid being slaves."[20] Many have said that the impact of popular commercial culture is so overwhelming that individuals must consciously choose to counteract it. Rodari chose to address how that might be done. Many others have connected that need for imagination with story and have come to the same conclusion. Jack Zipes, in *Creative Storytelling: Building Community, Changing Lives*, says that the development of imagination "is necessary, if we are to design our own lives" and he sees it almost as a guerrilla tactic to teach children how to counteract the advertising that their lives are steeped in.[21] It reminds one of Charles Darwin's statement that it is "not the strongest of the species that survives, nor the most intelligent, it is the one most adaptable to change."[22]

Another contemporary significance assigned to storytelling is its relationship with diversity and multiculturalism and other aspects of human connection. There is a hope that learning each other's stories will allow us to understand each other's values and perspectives. This is a real possibility if it is done with respect rather than shallowly or mechanically or with cynical "mining for intellectual capital."[23]

Beyond the "use" of story—for socialization, or education, or therapy—is the fact that it is primarily entertainment. The theatre of the mind's eye can go anywhere and requires no props, equipment, or batteries. It reclaims the human dimension in a time of commercialized techno-art. Excellent professional storytellers can mesmerize thousands in a concert, and, perhaps, with less glamor, but with just as much importance, stories can be shared one-on-one or with families or other groups.

Storytelling can build community, literally, for it is a shared experience that forms connections of a deep kind—not just an occasion of shared intellectual input but also of mutual emotional reaction to the story. As we become more and more diverse as a society, such occasions of shared, felt experience are really needed to build understanding. Storytelling is good not only for sharing the wealth of diversity but also for unifying that same diversity into a functioning whole. "My truths" and "your truths" can form not just a compromise but also a more complete and healthier whole. Years ago, I joked that New York was not a melting pot but more like a stew—with chunks of meat, potato, and different vegetables. Each chunk clings to its own discreet flavor, but the whole also has a distinct "stew" flavor, composed of their blending.

The impact of story on imagination has already been mentioned, but the stew metaphor re-introduces an aspect of analogy that deserves a little more attention. Many scientists have spoken of how they had suddenly understood something by seeing an analogy. There are many famous stories about this. For example, there is the story about James Watts watching a kettle as it boiled and lifted its lid and conceiving the idea of a steam engine. Another is of the recognition of the constitution of DNA as a double helix, with the sudden mental image of two snakes intertwined. Good minds need to be able to both originate and see connections and parallels. Einstein recognized this when he said that imagination was more important for scientists than knowledge.

Narrative thinking is, naturally enough, associated with oral styles of thinking. Story can be seen as the epitome of logic. Oral styles of thinking are no longer our only means, but we made a mistake in assuming that they were outmoded. Critical thinking skills are being recognized as less than automatic, and being able to deal with analogies is part of that package, as is sequencing and making causal connections. All of these are part of narrative thinking.

Rhetoric used to be one of the main skills one learned when getting an education. Not only did it fit one for a public life of politics and debate, but it also taught the logic of verbal thought. It is important to remember that logic developed in Greece, in a primarily oral culture. Walter Ong makes the point, in his *Orality and Literacy*, that the orally grounded education of young men being prepared for teaching, preaching, and other professions was replaced only very recently—long after writing and even printing were the norm—by the bookish commercially based education we accept as standard today.[24] He mentions the McGuffey readers as a case in point. Produced until after World War I, they were very heavily oral in focus, assuming that reading aloud was a primary goal fro readers, and that written language was primarily a means of transferring speech.[25] This was true both of the pedagogical content (e.g., breathing drills, pronunciation exercises) and the intellectual content (i.e., "heroic" material telling the kind of tale popular in told story, rather than that of the "Dick and Jane," realistic everyday accounts of later readers).

According to Ong, this abandonment of reading as an oral art betokens more than a passing fashion. It indicates a shift from communicating as a mutual act of conversation (or potential conversation, at least, even if it is a speech) to informing via media that go only one way, like print and the broadcast media. Even using pre-programmed interactive media is very different from conversation, for such programs are limited to what was programmed, and thus to the mind of the program designer rather than being the spontaneous, joint creation of two. (Anyone who has been frustrated by trying to use pre-prepared "Help" programs on the telephone will understand this point.)

Ong believes that our thought processes, personalities and social structures have all been affected, and that there have been real costs as well as benefits to our switching to print. It seems only sensible to try to hold on to the traditions that we still can, and to study what oral tradition is left, to reclaim at least some of those skills.[26]

One of the most disturbing conversations I have had recently was with an international reporter.[27] He said that one of the worst things about the destruction of the World Trade Center was being there and not being able to get any stories out of the people. They had stories but could not tell them well. It was not just that they were in shock. He had covered disasters elsewhere in the world and had gotten wonderful stories from survivors and victims. Regardless of their educational levels, most third world people still know how to tell stories, for story is part of their consciousness. Techno-literate people can only give depositions, not tell stories.

It was his further contention that the only storytellers left in the United States today are the police. No, not because of the many policemen with Irish roots, although, indeed that is one of the few European cultures that still has a sense of story, but because it is a career still learned largely by apprenticeship, and the stories are crucial. The camaraderie is largely built with shared stories, and it is very important when trust of one's "brothers" is absolutely necessary.

More important, much of what must be learned is really not something that can be written down—much of it is material that would cause major problems if it were "in print," anywhere, and much is what narrative is good for—giving principles to be taken to heart rather than rules to be followed. This is a good example of the analogy part of story. It is training for the instinct, not the intellect.

That is the issue, today. We really need to gain a sense of what narrative thinking is, so that is can be valued appropriately and so that we have a chance of passing it on to future generations at least somewhat intact. It is clear that much of this traditions and its skills is being lost and that this loss is a real detriment to society. Studies of body language have made it clear that much of a message is nonverbal. Surely the cues relating to tone and pitch and volume are also full of meaning, if we just studied them.

In the meantime, we need to be able to think and function well, orally. Regardless of one's political views, one needs to be able to express them so that others will understand and be able to agree or not based on the ideas and not just emotional reactions. One can still find statesmen who are coherent and articulate, even a few who are eloquent. That is worth keeping. It is equally important to have citizens who can listen critically and can discriminate between glib persuasion that reinforces our own opinions and truth, even when that truth is seen from a very different perspective. Intellectual integrity is a necessity, not a luxury in a democracy.

Economically, it is important to have people who can defend themselves against the hype of con-artists, be they local cardsharks or nationally advertised hucksters.

Personally, we all need proficiency with story. First of all, to tell our own stories—to both our own and others' ears. For it is what we tell ourselves about ourselves that gives us the basis on which, we build our lives. "Narrative maps the world and its inhabitants, including one's own position within that grid."[28] We also need to include story as a means of learning about the world from a variety of perspectives and as a means of picking up patterns of thinking that come with narrative: metaphor, sequence and consequence, humor, continuing on to the end, and other patterns.

Finally, we are entitled to enjoy our human heritage. Story has been part of being human as long as there has been a humanity to be part of. We need to recognize and be able to tell our own stories and those of the people we respect as well as to know traditional tales. Story can be valuable regardless of its medium, but just as pure air and water are needed in addition to air conditioning and sports drinks, so storytelling is needed in addition to film and television. Person-to-person, heart-to-heart storytelling is worth studying, not only for the content of its tales but also as a phenomenon, as an art, and as a means of communication. Story needs to be studied, and also to be held dear.

Notes

1. T.S.Eliot, Choruses from the play *The Rock*. (1934).

2. This reflects McLuhan's idea of the Medium is the Message in a new way. See Marshall McLuhan, *Understanding Media: The Extensions of Man* (New York: McGraw-Hill, 1964). Even information science is beginning to question this valuation. See, for example, Ronald E. Day, "The 'Conduit Metaphor' and The Nature and Politics of Information Studies," *Journal of the American Society for Information Science* 51 no. 9 (July 2000).

3. This is ignoring cartoons, of course, which do well at fantasy.

4. There was a reason that ancient Greek theatre used masks. It made the characters symbols rather than individuals.

5. One can only hope that alarmists are wrong in suggesting that real life is coming to copy such melodrama because audiences witnessing such behaviors take on the belief that such actions are appropriate expressions of their feelings.

6. The exceptions to that are the person who is so concerned with controlling things that fiction seems a waste of time rather than a revivifying type of intellectual play, or the person infected by our age's fear of sentiment and emotion; they are simply living their own scripts of fact-and-reason-based lives.

7. Lawrence Lessig, *Code: And Other Laws of Cyberspace* (New York: Basic Books, 1999).

8. Many storytellers have believed this. Thanks to Elizabeth Ellis for her clear discussions of this issue in her workshops.

9. Judaism, a religion based solidly on law, is also famous for its rabbis using stories. I pass on the recommendation of several Jewish storyteller friends to: *The Book of Legends Sefer Ha-Aggadah: Legends from the Talmud and Midrash*, edited by Hayim Nahman Bialik and Yehoshua Hana Ravnitzky, translated by William G. Braude (New York: Schocken, 1992).

10. For anyone interested in this aspect, I strongly recommend: Fran Stallings, "The Web of Silence: Storytelling's Power to Hypnotize," *The National Storytelling Journal* 5 no. 2 (Spring/Summer 1988). Available at: www.healingstory.org/articles/articles.html (6 June 2002). For a book on the how-to of healing and storytelling, *see* Nancy Mellon, *Storytelling and the Art of the Imagination* (Rockport, Mass.: Element, 1992) or Richard Stone, *The Healing Art of Storytelling: A Sacred Journey of Personal Discovery* (New York: Hyperion, 1996).

11. I heartily recommend Donna Haraway's book on the impact of technology on us as physical and emotional human beings. It is hard to read, though, be warned. Donna J. Haraway, *Modest Witness @Second_Millenium: FemaleMan©_Meets_Oncomouse™* (New York: Routledge, 1997).

12. A fascinating look at this can be found in Giorgio de Santillana and Hertha von Dechend, *Hamlet's Mill: An Essay Investigating the Origins of Human Knowledge and Its Transmission Through Myth* (Boston, Mass.: Godine, 1977 [1969]).

13. Michael LeBoeuf, PhD, *Imagineering: How to Profit from Your Creative Powers* (New York: Berkeley, 1986 [1980]), 11-12.

14. This is from a supplement written to: Egan, Kieran *Teaching as Storytelling: An Alternative Approach to Teaching and Curriculum in the Elementary School* (Chicago: University of Chicago Press, 1988), (London, Ontario: Althouse Press, 1986), 122. Available at: www.educ.sfu.ca/people/faculty/kegan/Supplement1.html   (7   July 2002).

15. A Position Statement from the Committee on Storytelling National   Council   of   Teacher   of   English.   Available   at: www.ncte.org/positions/teaching_storytelling.html (5 May 2002). Even New York State's new K-12 standards have recognized the importance of oral language for self expression and artistic expression.

16. "Anyone seeking success in the market of the future will have to be a storyteller. The story is the heart of the matter." Rolf Jensen, *The Dream Society: How the Coming Shift from Information to Imagination Will Transform Your Business* (New York: McGraw-Hill, 1999), 39.

17. Jensen, *Dream Society*, 52.

18. Jensen, *Dream Society*, 39.

19. Jensen, *Dream Society*, 52.

20. The full statement is:

Children must be given the opportunity to develop in various ways—in terms of their imagination, capacity for creative thought and ability to express themselves verbally and physically, with creative use of words, sounds and pictures. The purpose is not for them to become artists, but for them to avoid being slaves.

Gianni Rodari: *Grammatica della fantasia: Introduzione all'arte di inventare storie.* ("Grammar of Imagination") Turin, 1973. As translated by the Royal Danish Ministry of Foreign Affairs in their "The Power of Culture: The cultural dimension in development," © 2000. Available at:www.um.dk/danida/tpoc/chapter_3/3.5.asp (5 May 2002).

21. Jack Zipes, *Creative Storytelling: Building Community, Changing Lives* (New York: Routledge, 1995).

22. Charles Darwin, *Descent of Man*, (1871). Available at: ftp://ibiblio.org/pub/docs/books/Gutenberg/etext00/dsmn10.txt (5 June 2002).

23. This concern is a very real one, for many indigenous populations. A good explanation of Native American perspective can be found at: www.hanksville.org/sand/ (22 February 2002).

24. Walter Ong, *Orality and Literacy: The Technologizing of the Word.* (New York & London: Routledge, 1988 [1982]).

25. Walter Ong, *Orality and Literacy*, 116. For a further description of the McGuffey readers, try: www.nd.edu/~rbarger/www7/mcguffey.html (21 April, 2002).

26. Charles Darwin, in his *Descent of Man,* talked about the role of the voice and singing. It is rather amusing in this context:

> The impassioned orator, bard, or musician, when with his varied tones and cadences he excites the strongest emotions in his hearers, little suspects that he uses the same means by which his half-human ancestors long ago aroused each other's ardent passions, during their courtship and rivalry.

27. This came out in a discussion in a New York restaurant, some months after September 11, 2002. Two reporters (the one being quoted worked for Fox News Network) and I were at neighboring tables and got into a conversation over a book. We spent some time talking about storytelling.

28. Marsha Kinder, *Playing with Power in Movies, Television, and Video Games: From Muppet Babies to Teenage Mutant Ninja Turtles* (Berkeley,Calif.: University of California Press, 1991). Quoted in Zipes, *Creative Storytelling*, 202.

Chapter 3

Story as a Way of Making Meaning and Building Community

Introduction to the Talk

This was originally delivered at the School of Information Science and Policy State University of New York at Albany, New York, November 26, 2002.

I was invited to tell a story for the Capital Cities (Albany, New York) Telleration Event November 2002 and contacted a friend who had begun teaching for the School of Information and Policy of SUNY Albany. She immediately asked me to speak to her class and anyone else in the school who was interested. That invitation, combined with thoughts about how differently story and information science view "meaning," got this started.

Telling stories to adults at Telleration and then to children at local schools was fun. Following that by meeting an academic audience and watching them shift from listening to a lecture into the very different mode of story-listening convinced me yet again that we all need that balance between the strict logic of academe and the organic narrative wisdom of storytelling.

Story as a Way of Making Meaning
and Building Community

Experience is not so much what happens to us
as what we make of what happens to us.
                                    Aldous Huxley.[1]

In Huxley's sense, all of us create our own lives. Building with
the raw materials fate has given us, we are the architects of our
internal homes, our selves. The circumstances are given, but the
structures are our own. All humans do this constantly, whether
the stories we tell ourselves are about success and failure, right
and wrong, or whatever other scales form our value systems. Our
society does not ordinarily recognize the extent to which such
messages are based on story, but they are.

Our very sense of self is the story we tell of who we are and
who we are becoming. Throughout most of history, being human
was experienced in light of stories that carried the value of the
parent culture and were shared and reinforced among people in
the satisfying ritual of storytelling. The shared experience of storytelling still brings joy and gratification, both in the act of telling and in the activity of listening. More lastingly, the ideas that
come with the story can provide tools to build those constructed
internal lives and then to furnish and refurnish them. Such ideas
are not imposed on the hearers by the story but are enlivened
within them. George MacDonald got it right when he said:

> *It is there not so much to convey a meaning as to wake a*
> *meaning. . . . The best thing you can do for your fellow, .*
> *. . is—not to give him things to think about, but to wake*
> *things up that are in him; or say, to make him think*
> *things for himself.[2]*

That statement is very reminiscent of the statement attributed to
Socrates about a mind being not a jug to fill but a fire to light.

Becoming familiar with stories gives us the gift of understanding that situations can be interpreted in different ways, in
itself a basic element of wisdom. It also gives us the sense that

there are underlying patterns to events, patterns that we cannot always see from the middle of the action, but that will become clear at the end of the narrative. In other words, it gives us the hope of making meaning of our own lives as a kind of story.[3] This happens whether or not a given story is related to the listener's own situation—just by his absorbing the narrative pattern of story.

Sven Birkerts, the literary critic, speaks of this resonating with story as an act of the "secular soul." [4] When people speak of story as a form of healing, this is often what is meant. How does it work? It enables the individual to view things from different perspectives rather than being trapped in a single way of seeing and it teaches patience about waiting until the end to see "what really happens."

There is a wonderful story from China that demonstrates this:

There was once a peasant who owned a stallion. It was his proudest and most valuable possession. One spring day it ran away, and people from the village came to commiserate, "Oh, what bad luck. What a shame."

"Well, thank you for your sympathy, but we'll just have to wait and see," replied the peasant.

Only a few days later, the stallion returned, and brought with him several wild mares. The peasant's neighbors now came to offer congratulations: "Oh, such good luck."

Once again, the peasant replied: Well, thank you for your congratulations, but we'll just have to wait and see."

Not long after the stallion's return, the man's son tried to mount one of the new mares, and she threw him off, leaving him with a broken leg. People from the village came to commiserate, "Oh, what bad luck. Now your boy won't be able to help you with the plowing. What a shame"

"Well, thank you for your sympathy, but we'll just have to wait and see," replied the peasant.

When the fall came, and with it the harvest, the boy was still limping badly, so he could not do his share of the work with gathering in the crops. Then, just as people were offering their sympathies, along came a press gang from the army that took all the young men of the village off to fight a war. All, that is, but the lame boy.

All the neighbors came to complain about the loss of their sons and congratulate the peasant father on the safety of his son. The peasant replied: "Well, thank you for your congratulations, but we'll just have to wait and see!"

Learning to react honestly to things that happen, while recognizing that each experience is only one part of a larger picture, is a valuable lesson.

Please grant me some of that patience while I go in some unexpected directions, beginning with the idea of viewing things in various ways. Consider the many different ways there are to map the same territory. The one we think of first is the road map, which is the most common. There are also topographic maps, showing the hills and valleys and waterways. There are political maps, showing town boundaries, and political maps showing various election districts—and maps showing where polling stations are for election day. There are school district maps, showing catchment areas for the schools. There are historical maps showing "where" a spot *used* to be—for example, Beverwyck rather than Albany, or New Amsterdam rather than New York. There are maps showing library branches; maps showing church parishes; supermarkets in a particular chain; maps of Starbucks and McDonald's stores. One friend who flies has maps showing airports, while another who sails has maps that show where harbors and public docks are. All of these are factually accurate. All are true. All cover the same area. But each looks quite different.

If one were in the desert in the summer, with a broken car and no cell phone, a map showing water holes would be of more use than a road map. If one were in the same spot with a working car during a winter rainstorm, a map showing where there were flood-passable roads and safe arroyo crossings would be worth more than the water hole map. In other words, all the maps may be correct, but the "right" map depends on the occasion and purpose. Similarly, a story may be told from a particular point of view or "map." More often, though, it is told from a place of omniscience that presents the overall theme or meaning, like a "master map," and may or may not express individual characters' perspectives.

Each of us has the ability to choose and to create our maps, defining the territories of our lives. This was what the psychiatrist and philosopher Victor Frankl was talking about when he spoke of the last freedom—the freedom to make meaning of our own lives. He spoke of the most desperate of situations, the concentration camps of World War II, but it is equally true of times of joy. He believed that both Freud's idea, that human life is based on instinctual drives, and Adler's, that it was based on the drive for power, were both wrong. He held that:

> Man's search for meaning is the primary motivation in his life and not a "secondary rationalization" of instinctual drives. This meaning is unique and specific in that it must and can be fulfilled by him alone; only then does it achieve a significance which will satisfy his own *will* to meaning. There are some authors who contend that meanings and values are "nothing but defense mechanisms, reaction formations and sublimations." But as for myself, I would not be willing to live merely for the sake of my "defense mechanisms," nor would I be ready to die merely for the sake of my "reaction formations." Man, however, is able to live and even to die for the sake of his ideals and values![5]

It is not just the old question about whether you view the glass as half empty or half full, although that is a big part of it. The other part is "why," and "so what," and these require awareness of a sense of meaning. We most commonly accept meaning from outside sources, but it is entirely optional whether we define ourselves in terms of belief systems, codes of behavior, brands purchased, jobs held or social roles with which we choose to identify. In other words, we choose those stories we tell to define ourselves, whether adopted from the outside or internally authored.

Following that map analogy, let's try a parallel one. Think of America and the car. It started out as a great invention to get from one place to another and enabled us to move out of the immediate neighborhood of our families and, yet, stay fairly close to them in terms of time—a real boon in a pioneer culture which encouraged moving on. It also enabled us to take jobs beyond walking distance and provided broad choices in high school education by enabling school districts to take advantage of economies of scale.

The way this has developed is that we are now spread out very thinly. We do not have cousins to play with next door, but have to set up play dates or plan trips to see them. We do not have neighborhood groups playing kick-the-can or inventing their own games and learning to figure out and follow their own, mutually developed, rules. Instead there are huge, economy-sized schools where one can get lost, and organized sports and dance classes—to which the child must be chauffeured. The village neighborhood just does not exist anymore, with its sense of shared community and mores.[6] The old village perspective of shared responsibility for raising children has been replaced with professional childcare specialists.

Commuting to work has become a lengthy, distressing business. Commutes of more than an hour are considered quite normal, and this has changed us into creatures that consider cars a kind of personal space/moving home, filled with electronic connectivity providing music and news via radio or backseat video and outreach via CB radio or cell phone, so that we do not have to be "out of touch" during travel time. Mugs are designed to fit cupholders and keep coffee hot. There is nothing inherently bad about this, but it does mean that car trips are no longer special occasions for family stories and discussions.

All of this geographic stretching means that our loyalties are spread out, and, perhaps by the very nature of our emotional makeup, become thinner. As we become more and more peripatetic, we become almost rootless. We are born in one place, to parents who came from someplace else; we move a few more times with our family before it is time to "move away from home" to college; then we find a job and start to put down ties of our own—to be ripped up when we start changing jobs and start the cycle anew. The average person now moves more than once every five years. About the only ones who seem to stay fixed are the small number of rural families connected to a particular piece of land, and those from families rich enough to afford family estates lasting through generations. It is as if we have become a kind of capitalist migrant labor—fruit pickers following the business seasons. This is as true of academics as of corporate employees and military personnel, by the way; today's ivory towers come with wheels. One of the less fortunate results of this is that we learn to leave rather than to try to solve problems—the ruin and run response.

This moving around is not like that of the Rom (also called Gypsies or Travelers), who take their communities and culture (including stories), and, thus, their roots, with them. Prejudice used to be aimed at such nomadic groups because their loyalty is to their group rather than to the communities passed through. Their situation is worth considering in relation to the general population as it too becomes less fixed and loosens traditional moorings—but without taking its community along. To what do contemporary people feel loyal? Robert Putnam, in his *Bowling Alone,* addressed the topic of our loss of the sense of shared responsibility that was felt by individuals in stable communities. This, along with the mutual trust it builds, allows for a sense of generalized reciprocity, and forms *social capital.* He said:

> A society characterized by generalized reciprocity is more efficient than a distrustful society, for the same reason that money is more efficient than barter. If we don't have to balance every exchange instantly, we can get a lot more accomplished. Trustworthiness lubricates social life. Civic engagement and social capital entail mutual obligation and responsibility for action. . . . social networks and norms of reciprocity can facilitate cooperation for mutual benefit.[7]

Having defined social capital, he then begins to describe the ways in which it is unraveling in our country as we become less and less engaged with others (as seen in lowering attendance at everything from religious groups to card parties to voting booths).

To get back to the car analogy, though, what about our relationship to the land that we now drive so quickly past? Notice that I said driving past, not driving through. Our highways are designed to make getting from place to place as speedy and efficient as possible. Time pressures are so great that travel time seems a waste of time rather than an entertainment in itself. The countryside and communities in between end points are seen as an impediment to "getting there." The traveler feels like a customer, not a guest, when stopping on the road. Tourists are concerned with getting *to* a spot rather than with taking a trip as a form of vacation in itself. Gone is the old idea of a journey of exploration to "see the countryside" that came complete with stories about family members and even folktales and urban legends to pass the time and, incidentally, practice communication skills.

The geographic world provided a concrete example, but the information world is a little closer to the point. Birkerts[8] addresses the same concern in a parallel way. He fears that, as we become more and more overwhelmed with data and intertwined and interconnected electronically, we are becoming shallower and shallower in our approach to that data. He feels that there must be a choice between depth and breadth, and as a culture we are choosing breadth of overview rather than depth of understanding. Quantity has replaced quality. Something similar can be seen in our reaction to the news. Only so much news can be taken in before we become jaded by the tragedies it so often contains.

We need ways to reconnect meaningfully with other humans, at least some of the time. This is true of us as individuals and as a culture. Story was a traditional means for doing this and can be of assistance again.

Similarly, as family structure changes, and families form, dissolve and reform as stepfamilies, we must make connections within those families. Beyond those families, we must connect with others who are likeminded, to form communities based on mutual beliefs and understandings. One proven way to do this is by learning each other's stories.

For those who need science-based statements before paying attention, I recommend the book *A General Theory of Love*. The authors, three professors of psychiatry, offer a call of alarm because the emotional brain is not being properly developed and supported in our society. They provide a biological basis for their statements. Their preface declares that:

> where intellect and emotion clash, the heart often has the greater wisdom. In a pleasing turnabout, science—Reason's right hand—is proving this so. The brain's ancient emotional architecture is not a bothersome animal encumbrance. Instead it is nothing less than the key to our lives. [9]

They are not focused on narrative, any more than Robert Putnam is, but their work is relevant to the issues that make story important now, and they also give an explanation for how storytelling actually works, by explaining what we know so far of the *limbic brain,* that is, the physical part of the brain that deals with emotion and connection. They say:

> Because limbic states can leap between minds, feelings are contagious, while notions are not . . . the limbic activity of those around us draws our emotions into almost immediate congruence . . . it's the *crowd* that releases storytelling magic, the essential, communal, multiplied wonder. [10]

They later say:

> The limbic brain is an emotional magnet. . . . Our minds are in turn pulled by the emotional magnets of those close to us, transforming any landscape we happen to contemplate and painting it with the colors and textures *they* see. [11]

In terms of society, they question the values of the information age and its tools:

> A child's electronic stewards—television, videos, computer games—are the emotional equivalent of bran; they occupy attention and mental space without nourishing. An ironic revelation of the television-computer age is that what people want from machines is humanity: stories, contact, and interaction. . . . Today's machines deliver not limbic connections but imprecise simulations. . . . However enticing their entertainment

value, mechanical companions are unworkable relationship substitutes for adults and children alike.[12]

. . . People who cannot *see* content must settle for appearances.
. . . When a society loses touch with limbic bedrock, spin wins. Substantive aspirations inevitably suffer.[13]

What is the connection of this concern for social change with storytelling? A fair question. As we disconnect from traditional roots and communities that gave us meaning in terms of relationships with others in that community, it is crucial that we develop individual internal roots of meaning that can go with us. We need to feel a connection to humanity as a whole, not just the community "we grew up in." And we are being asked to do this just at a time when other parts of that human family are making it very clear that they hate America, in part because they blame America for the kinds of changes that we have just been discussing.

It is clear that we all need to grow up fairly quickly, and become mature enough to deal with things as they happen. We will have to be individually responsible, if the peer pressures of community lessen and no longer provide control over people's behavior. We will have to be very flexible as the rules and tools of our world keep changing. It is good to keep in mind that what Darwin really said was that *adaptability* was the key to a species' survival. Combining Darwin's thought with the assumption that reading is good for children because they will grow literate, brings to mind what Alvin Toffler said back in the 1970s: "The illiterate of the 21st century will not be those who cannot read and write, but those who cannot learn, unlearn, and relearn."[14]

Storytelling is not a panacea, but it is a proven way to begin to address some of these issues.[15] It means developing storytelling as part of what communities still exist; encouraging and supporting existing tellers and letting organizations and communities become aware of the resources that already exist. Corporations, schools, museums, libraries, parks, religious groups, resorts, and recreational centers, should all have tellers on retainer, just as they have legal counsel. Not just for entertainment, or to provide propaganda supporting the institution, but to also take the traditional role of fool, for example, challenging the status quo with questions.

In addition to setting up situations where people can become comfortable with storytelling so that their appetite for more stories develops, it means growing tellers. That means teaching talented individuals to become storytellers for groups, and teaching everyone to be able to see his or her own life as a story, and to be able to tell it well enough to be understood. To be *able* to tell it, mind, not to be forced to do so. Sometimes one wants to be understood by others, and sometimes one's story is only for internal consumption.

What is it about storytelling that is so valuable? Another fair question. First, listening to stories develops the imagination, by requiring the hearer to join with the teller in creating the story within his or her own mind's eye. Second, it teaches critical thinking skills, such as cause and effect. Third, it teaches moral thinking—not in terms of rules, but in terms of guidelines, teaching principles that can be adapted to the reality of shifting situations—learning the spirit of the law rather than the letter. Biblical Solomon typifies this kind of judgment, which was the best available for millennia, and which seems to be reappearing in the guise of television shows á la *Judge Judy*, in which justice is based on personal judgment rather than law. Fourth, story makes abstract issues feel personal, and thus understandable, and create an impact on each individual listener. For instance, I have learned more about history and the danger of prejudice from stories told by people I know about their personal experience of racial prejudice in America and in Nazi Germany than from my historical reading or from lectures about "facts." Fifth, and finally, myth seems to be the language of our subconscious, and that is not going to change, no matter how technologized we become. To quote the three psychiatrists one last time: "Ideas bounce like so many peas off the sturdy incomprehension of the limbic and reptilian brain. The dogged implicitness of emotional knowledge, its relentless unreasoning force, prevents logic . . ."[16] The question today is whether we will continue to maintain the mythic material of humankind on the grassroots individual and community level, as it has been through the ages, or allow that need to be colonized completely by the techno-wizardry of power-based shows and games produced by commercial interests.

All five of these essentials are shared with print story, but there are additional values unique to the experience of sharing storytelling. Most important of all, in my eyes, the experience builds community by establishing the trust of shared creation. A bond is created between teller and all who listen. Elizabeth Ellis tells of a group of listeners who have remained connected ever since she responded to a request at a story concert for her to repeat her telling of the Greek myth of the Goddess Demeter seeking her daughter Persephone in the underworld. That request came not long after Ellis had herself gone through fearing that her daughter was dead, and looking for her in the Dallas morgue. Her experience impacted her telling in such a way that each hearer's consciousness was affected and the audience bonded so that years later they still recognized each other. [17] Such an occasion may represent an extreme case, granted, but the bonding experience is common, for storytelling is a community experience, not just an individual one, as reading is; there are others to share the reaction, be it tears of sorrow, of rage, or of laughter.

That trust building, and bond building, based on shared thought and shared intellectual play, is extremely important as we become less attached to specific settings. It is every bit as important as the shared physical play of neighborhood friends or fraternity brothers in forming who we are as local community. Shared story is even more important in developing a sense of community that can survive our mobile lifestyle and be available to connect with new groups. It is not a coincidence that community and communications come from the same Latin root. They both involve the *sharing* of ideas.

Perhaps it is not surprising that both concepts are undergoing such change. After all, more than our lifestyle has changed. Who would have thought of "virtual communities" a few decades ago; yet now the phrase is commonplace. The language itself is changing as the media using it change. Language changed radically as print became the established means of communicating ideas and stories and it is changing again. Recently, "connection" referred to human relationships, now the immediate assumption is that it refers to electronic connectivity. "Communications" now is primarily associated with technology rather than individual conversation.[18]

Both of these references, to changes in local community and to those in speech, are relevant, for they prompt thoughts of how we live life and why we need story on a daily level, not just "out there" on the screen but with the human connection of live story-telling. It is not just that body language and tone convey more than print or electronic words, but the very presence of another human being matters. Birkerts begins talking about a human "aura" that is only there in the real time, real space of a person's presence. Whether or not that exists, it is clear that there is a great difference between the real thing and virtual reality. Why else do people get excited at seeing a movie star in real life walking down the street, when what they do on the screen is infinitely more impressive? Why else do people go to shopping malls to be waited on rather than just buying online? Why else do students confirm that watching a videotaped telling of a story is infinitely less satisfying than hearing it live.

It is this difference that we are discussing, ill defined as it is. It is more than establishing eye contact, although that is part of it. There is a palpable difference of feeling in the room. Many have discussed this storytelling "shared trance." Describing it is like the proverbial attempt to describe the taste of a strawberry. The closest I can come is to contrast the way it is so easy to take a nap in a room where there are sleeping cats—as opposed to one in which a person is sitting silent but angry. Maybe someday we will discover that we do interact upon each other via rays or pheromones or something, but at least science now recognizes that the limbic parts of our brains do act on each other.[19] In the meantime, we can try to set it up as a positive influence. We can set up the habit of seeing shared story experience as group situations of shared trust and meaning, to counteract those of competition or selling/being sold.

The other reason for pushing in-person storytelling is that it establishes that ordinary people can carry and share wisdom. It does not matter whether the experience is shared one-on-one or in groups, it is proof that real, living people like you and me can share important thoughts, not just figures on the screen or authors. That subliminal message is crucial to convey to children, who are inundated with highly polished professionally produced data and entertainment. The question "is that story true?," which comes more and more frequently, is really a symptom of the fact that the child recognizes that here is something important, but does not know where to fit the experience into his or her scheme of things that matter.

Most story now is being provided by the commercial entertainment industry. Being sold does not make such story products evil, but it is important to recognize that the goal of the manufacturer/teller is selling merchandise, and that requires selling to appetite. They are responsible to investors rather than to society, so developing "good taste" or "good citizenship" or any of the other qualities that democracy was expected to build for all cannot be left to such story-products. It is not just our bodies that are reacting to junk food diets.

By listening to stories, children are developing the capability that they need to become real readers rather than just decoders of print data; to become thinkers who can interpret another's words into alternative realities, consider the validity of those ideas, and then follow those up with ideas of their own. They are learning that story can be a source of meaning. They are also learning to consider story in general, and whether to trust a particular story or not. The world is going to need these minds more and more. We want children who can trust as well as reject stories that don't "ring true." Earlier generations learned to distrust the story in the ads found on the back of comic books for "magic decoder rings" and lessons that would teach you to be safe from bullies kicking sand in your face. We want to provide the equivalent of that bully protector, by teaching children to assess the myriad messages flying at them hourly. This generation must learn to sift quickly, without automatically discounting everything just because doing so takes less effort and offers less risk of looking gullible and thus weak. Armor plate may protect, but it also prevents a free life.

If building community, growing a future of imaginative minds that can deal with the consequences of the techno-future, and providing a living, word-of-mouth link for ideas that are not related to the consumer culture, are not enough, there is one more point. Stories are our strongest link, beyond our DNA, with humankind throughout history; in fact some have called story a kind of DNA of the mind and spirit, for it runs deep, deep into the past of our ancestors. As we become more and more linked to the electronic world, and relate less and less to anything from the past, our stories become more and more crucial if we are not to become as emotionally rootless as we are becoming physically disconnected.

Just as whole grains and vegetables remain available as healthy foods, even when convenience food is faster, cheaper, and easier, so ancient stories still speak to our subconscious in nourishing ways and provide for many different "recipes" for meaning. It could be that our psychological health will be saved by that nourishment, in spite of the empty calories of commercial popular culture and the intellectual pollution of too much information.

There is considerable irony in the lack of storytelling in our current world that so anxiously seeks pleasure, for it is very enjoyable. It may not be as effortless or flashily attention getting as a flickering screen, but on the other hand it does not need great discipline—it just asks that someone be present. Even media-gorged children respond with enthusiasm, once they experience it, and adults who have the self-discipline it requires to turn off the screen enjoy it also. It does not even require a fortune to produce.

The problem is that storytelling is not understood. Too few groups join together—without specific goals to accomplish in limited amounts of time—to welcome storytelling. Too many narcissistic people who want to talk about themselves have turned us off from tellers of personal stories. Too many boring amateurs wanting attention have tried to tell us jokes and stories. Too many of us stopped hearing stories with the end of the bedtime stories of early childhood and have come to think of listening to stories as something to be outgrown by the time you learn to read.[20] Too many of us have established patterns of seeking the stories ready-made in popular culture that offer the satisfaction of being in sync with the world while feeding the appetite for story. Too many of us fed on such stories have learned that they provide entertainment without meaning and have come to dismiss that underlying hunger for meaning in story, just the way we have learned to let watching television with canned laughter pass for sharing a joke among a group of friends.

In spite of this, a renaissance of storytelling is definitely underway, as can be seen in the National Storytelling Festival and Tellabration, which is now international, and the fact that there are many professional tellers, several of whom make good livings at it. Because it requires no technology, it is a way of maintaining the dignity and meaning of human beings unadorned with technology. It is a direct antidote to the sense of powerlessness of the individual in the electronic tribal hive. One person can demonstrate depth and carry others with him, and do it pleasurably.

Storytelling provides proof that we can, in the same life, if not at the same moment, be both connected by our equipment and float alone in the cosmos of timelessness. If we are to give up more and more privacy, then we must go more deeply inward to build and maintain self; the space we need to build is not the external virtual world of technology but the private inner world of what literary critic Birkerts called "secular soul,"[21] what others might call "character". He says that novels deepen our sense of self as we add other's stories to our own experience. That is definitely true, but the reality is that, long before print and the novel, that function was performed by the told story, and it drew people together, rather than separating them as solitary reading does.

That sense of timelessness, "Dreamtime," as the Aborigines of Australia call it, is not the same as historical time, nor the same as virtual cyberspace and cybertime. The difference is that it is physically shared, and, thus, feeds our need to feel part of a community, and provides communally shared nourishment. It expands our horizons internally. As we become more frenetic in our multi-tasking, and risk becoming "human doings" rather than human beings, it becomes more and more important as a balance, if not as an antidote.

So, this ends with a plea: seek out good stories, share them, listen to them and encourage others to listen and tell. If you want to think of fighting the good fight for coherence and critical thinking; if you want to join in the struggle for spiritual growth as part of a religious tradition or as part of the new age interest in ancient beliefs and healing; if you want to help people develop imagination and creativity; if you want to reframe your own story by retelling it from a new perspective; or if you just want to wallow in the pleasure of being in the land of wonder—go to it. The water is fine, and there is room for all.

Notes

1. A fuller version of the quote (discussing science fiction) is:

Experience is not a matter of having actually swum the Helle-spont, or danced with the dervishes, or slept in a doss-house. It is a matter of sensibility and intuition, of seeing and hearing the significant things, of paying attention at the right moments, of understanding and co-ordinating. Experience is not what happens to a man; it is what a man does with what happens to him.

From the introduction to Aldous Huxley, *Texts and Pretexts: an Anthology with Commentaries* (London: Chatto & Windus, 1932).

2. George MacDonald, "The Fantastic Imagination," from *A Dish of Orts*. (Reprint. Whitethorne, Calif.: Johannesen, 1996. [1893]) 321. Available at: www.gmsociety.org.uk/ 28 September 2002). (The ellipsed phrase was "next to rousing his conscience".)

3. Sven Birkerts had this to say about the phenomenon:

. . . there is a very special transformation that takes place when we read fiction that is not experienced in nonfiction. This transformation, or catalyzing action, can be seen to play a vital part in what we might call, grandly, existential self-formation," 91.

"Even when the awareness of meaning or the sense of fated-ness were not to be gathered from my surroundings, novels gave me the grounds, the incentive, to live *as if.* Indeed, more than anything else, reading created in me the awareness that life could be lived and known as a unified whole; that the patterns which make meaning are disclosed gradually," 94.

Sven Birkerts, *Gutenberg Elegies: The Fate of Reading in an Electronic Age* (New York: Fawcett Columbine, 1994).

4. "The time of reading, the time defined by the author's language resonating in the self, is not the world's time, but the soul's. I don't know how else to define the soul in secular terms except as a kind of self-consistent condensation of the self," 85.

5. Viktor E. Frankl, *Man's Search for Meaning: An Introduction to Logotherapy*, Third edition (New York: Touchstone/Simon & Schuster, 1984), 105. He also mentioned a study of the National Institute of Mental Health which found 78 percent of students saying "finding a purpose and meaning to my life," was very important to them, while only 16 percent checked "making a lot of money." No date was given, beyond the implication that it was recent in 1984, but it would be interesting to find out if that ratio were different today.

6. It is only fair to add that the less savory elements of gossip, and so forth, are also gone.

7. Robert Putnam addressed this in his *Bowling Alone: The Collapse and Revival of American Community* (New York: Simon &Schuster/Touchstone, 2001 [2000]), 21.

8. Birkerts, *Gutenberg Elegies*.

9. Thomas Lewis, Fari Amini, and Richard Lannon, *A General Theory of Love* (New York: Vintage, 2000), viii.

10. Lewis, *Love*, 64 (they were talking about films, but it is even more true of live storytelling, for it is a group connection of creation, not just passive observing).

11. Lewis, *Love*, 163.

12. Lewis, *Love*, 198.

13. Lewis, *Love*, 211.

14. Alvin Toffler, *Future Shock* (New York: Harcourt Brace, 1970).

15. Live drama can do the same thing, but it is extremely expensive, in comparison to storytelling which can be done without props, theatres, full casts, and so on. Clearly, this does not mean commercially videotaping and telecasting great storytellers, either, at the exclusion of local telling.

16. Lewis, *Love*, 118.

17. This story is included in a CD, taped at the National Storytelling Festival. Elizabeth Ellis, *Mothers and Daughters, Daughters and Mothers* (Dallas, Tex.: New Moon Productions, 2001).

18. This is discussed in: Tor Nørretranders, *The User Illusion: Cutting Consciousness Down to Size*. Translated by Jonathan Sydenham (New York: Viking, 1998 [1991]).

19. Having twice been in situations where groups began to panic (one was a theatre fire that was quickly extinguished and explained to the audience just as people were starting to flee, the other was a thun-

derstorm over a crowd, with the only way out a small underpass and the first there not wanting to leave its shelter so that the huge wave of people pressing from behind could come through), I can attest to the fact that one physically reacts to crowd moods of alarm.

20. If you don't know Jim Trelease's *The Read-Aloud Hand-book.* Fifth edition. (New York: Penguin, 2001 [1982]), it is worth tracking down. He explains why and how it is so important.

21. Sven Birkets, *The Gutenberg Elegies: The Fate of Reading in an Electronic Age* (New York: Fawcett/Columbine, 1994 [1991]).

Chapter 4

Reading as Work,
Story as Play

Introduction to the Talk

This was originally delivered to the New York Congress of Parents and Teachers. Parents as Reading Partners. Melville, New York. October 20, 1999.

A former student recommended me to Parents as Reading Partners, a group supporting adults as they help children become enthusiastic readers. I was asked to provide a workshop on storytelling and that was a success, so I was invited to provide the key-note address to the same group the next year. Because I believe very much in what they do, but I am also conscious that pushing reading too hard could backfire, I was prompted to write Reading as Work/Story as Play.

Reading as Work,
Story as Play

It is hardly surprising that children should enthusiastically start their education at an early age with the Absolute Knowledge of computer science; while they are unable to read, for reading demands making judgments at every line. . . . Conversation is almost dead, and soon so too will be those who knew how to speak.

Guy Debord [1]

Guy Debord, the French Situationist philosopher who said this is just one of the many people who believe reading is important, and that, for a variety of reasons, it is endangered. This very group, Parents as Reading Partners (PARP) would not have come into being without a concern for reading. The warning that I want to make is that as we push its importance, we may be making reading external and task oriented, rather than an integral part of the person. I fear that what we have done best in our schools is to teach children that reading is work. We encourage reading to pass tests and to prepare yourself to earn a living, instead of making it seem like a combined passport and driver's license that allows you to travel a path to enjoyment and personal fulfillment as well as commute to work. We don't reward children for playing, or for learning to drive—but we do for eating vegetables and for reading.

Somehow literacy's role has been switched. At the beginning of public education, literacy was seen as a gift, the key to sharing knowledge and the excitement of stories. The connection with job hunting was secondary for earlier generations of learners. You became a full person, and thus someone worth hiring, not just someone who was capable of pushing papers. That has changed and education now is marketed as the way to a good job.

As for access to the world of fiction—now our stories are served up readymade in films, with no visualizing imagination needed, so we don't need reading anymore for entertainment. Reading for pleasure seems pointless to many people, just as baking a cake from scratch does, when one can get a perfectly good cake from Sara Lee or Entemann's without all the bother or effort and not a great deal of difference in cost.

It is clear that we are developing a serious problem, not just with *illiteracy*, for example, the inability to read, but also with *a-literacy*, which is the choice not to read. PARP exists precisely to counteract this pattern among our children, but I feel some anxiety about the sub-text of the messages that are being dealt out. Earlier I mentioned the problems of encouraging reading by offering rewards that ends up teaching that reading needs an external payoff, when the truth is that reading becomes its own reward, just as driving does. The problem is that this is true only *after* the initial investment of learning to read easily has already been made. Many attractive alternatives are calling, in the meantime, so for those not already committed to the idea of reading, there is a dangerously vulnerable stage when the exciting novelty of learning to read has worn off and the process of decoding has not yet become automatic enough that one can spin off and concentrate on the content.

Encouragement may be needed during this long transitional phase, but at the same time, supporting this process must be done carefully. Why then is this just the moment when we begin demanding book reports about content and start standardized testing to increase the stress? Why is this the moment we start literary analysis and force children to read to find themes, and perform other analytical tasks, instead of just reading and allowing reading to become a desirable activity?

If it is important to teach literary elements and analysis, why don't we have children watch videos of sitcoms and add homework to that watching by having them write about video as drama? The lesson content would be as effective, and the situation might make children look at such things with a little less unquestioning acceptance. It would also make reading a pleasurable escape, instead of unpleasant work. The old patterns, developed when reading was the only option, no longer work except with children who are already committed readers. We have accepted the reality of the internet in teaching, why still live in denial of television as the main medium of entertainment?

Perhaps teachers (and parents) have put such work themselves into learning how to *teach* reading that they have, consciously or unconsciously, come to see it primarily as work. It is discouraging to see how many soon-to-be teachers groan at "all the books they are expected to read" for a children's literature class, instead of feeling glee at having justification for spending lots of time immersed in great stories. No wonder the children taught by such teachers search avidly for the shortest books. How could anyone teach the joy of reading without feeling it first?

I remember a friend, who, incidentally, *did* grow up to be a reader, telling me how she learned to read. She was in Catholic school in the 1950s, and a note went home saying that she was not doing well in reading and was in danger of failing the first grade. Her mother and aunt decided that this needed to be corrected, and so she was tutored at home by a very simple method. She was forced to read aloud, and each time she read a word wrong her hair was pulled, hard. Eventually she came to recognize all the words in her readers—but out of self-defense rather than enjoyment or pride in accomplishment. Fortunately, she wanted to read and her ego was already strong, so there was a happy ending, but this could hardly be recommended as an effective method for others with learning disabilities.

Knowing both the girl and the mother in this story, I find it amazing, but it is true. I mention it because the parent's anxiety about having a non-reading child is so clear. Today, that mother's behavior would be recognized as abusive, but how often is that same wish to create readers risked by those working to develop the skill but ignoring and thus dissolving the budding personal connection between the young reader and book? It is *not* just an intellectual connection, but an emotional one. I still remember how many books were spoiled for me in school by being forced to write book reports or answer analytical questions. And, remember, this was a child who was already committed to reading. Sharing a book is one thing, but too often the impulse to teach can become a kind of intellectual invasion of privacy, like friends who are parents of teenagers trying to set up a romance between their children and then quizzing them about the date. Setting up occasions when their children meet is fair game, but forcing a relationship and then snooping is something else.

The intellectual part of reading is, of course, the primary aspect; the physical part is just the means to the end. The theorist Wolfgang Iser spoke of *The Act of Reading*[2] as being an equation. The text is central, but what the *reader* brings to the text in the act of reading is as important as what the author brought, for it is only in the *combination* of that text and the reader's mind that each individual act of reading comes to fruition. To be obvious: a book written in Chinese does little for someone who does not read Chinese, no matter how brilliant the author or the reader. Iser, of course, was referring to far more subtle and complex issues of connotation in the equation. I would like to offer, as an example, the experience one of my students had as a seventh grader. She read *Animal Farm*,[3] and it was the one thing that made that year bearable, for she was new to the school and found herself the only African American in a Catholic girls' school filled with girls who considered themselves much "more equal" than she.[4] To this day, *Animal Farm* is about racism to her although the author was writing about Communism. Further, since hearing her story, my experience of the book is now affected, secondhand. Sharing books is not just an intellectual experience, but is saturated with human feeling. As Voltaire is quoted as saying: "It is with books as with the fires in our grates: everybody borrows a light from his neighbor to kindle his own, which is in turn communicated to others, and each partakes of all."[5]

One of my favorite science fiction writers, Orson Scott Card, in an introduction to a later edition of his *Ender's Game*, shared his musings on the way readers responded so deeply to the book. He wrote:

> These readers found that *Ender's Game* was not merely a "mythic" story, dealing with general truths, but something much more personal: to them *Ender's Game* was an epic tale, a story that expressed who they are as a community, a story that distinguished them from the other people around them. . . . The truth of the story was not truth in general, but *their* truth.
>
>   . . . Stories can be read so differently—even clear stories, even stories that deliberately avoid surface ambiguities.
> . . . Why else do we read fiction, anyway? Not to be impressed by somebody's dazzling language—or at least I hope that's not our reason. I think most of us, anyway, read these stories that we know are not "true" because we're hungry for another kind of truth: The mythic truth about human nature in general, the particular truth about those life-communities that define our own identity, and the most specific truth of all: our own self-story. Fiction, because it is not about somebody who actually lived in the real world, always has the possibility of being about ourself.
>   . . . All of these uses are valid; all these readings of the book are "correct." For all these readers have placed themselves inside this story, not as spectators, but as participants, and so have looked at the world of *Ender's Game*, not with my eyes only, but also with their own.
>   This is the essence of the transaction between storyteller and audience. The "true" story is not the one that exists in my mind; it is *certainly* not the written words on the bound paper that you hold in your hands. The story in my mind is nothing but a hope; the text of the story is the tool I created in order to try to make that hope a reality. The story itself, the true story, is the one that the audience members create in their minds, guided and shaped by my text, but then transformed, elucidated, expanded, edited, and clarified by their own experience, their own desires, their own hopes and fears.
>   The story of *Ender's Game* is not this book, though it has that title emblazoned on it. The story is one that you and I will

construct together in your memory. If the story means anything to you at all, then when you remember it afterward, think
of it, not as something I created, but rather as something that
we made together. [6]

Taking this in a slightly different direction, one which I consider crucial—it is not just the life experience the reader brings
to the book that creates the reading, but his or her imaginative
capability. This ability to visualize is something that must be developed like any other creative skill. Morten Vildgaas said, *"You
are the author of everything you read between the lines."*[7] If one
is not comfortable creating the set and peopling it with the characters as a theater of the mind, reading is going to be hard, boring work, not enjoyable, exciting entertainment.

Birkerts wrote a fine article on children's reading and listening, and commented on the difference between the reading of
children and that of adults:

> When we first begin to read as children, we carry out the as-
> tonishing and, yes, Godlike task of creating the world from
> print. That is, we discover and affirm in ourselves the power
> of being able to do this, and most of our early reading is, sig-
> nificantly, about mastering this power.[8]

This ability to imagine is what is so important in reading and
in other creative endeavors. It is a natural development in
children, but cannot be taken for granted. Listening to stories has
been accepted as part of that development until very recently in
human history, when it was first augmented with written
literature that expanded told story and language beyond the
physical presence of the teller, and is now being supplanted by
visual media.

We are in danger, as a society, of losing the ability to imagine. Think of another ability we also take for granted—learning
to walk. Parents offer encouragement, but do no more, for learning to walk is automatic. If however, a child were kept in a
wheelchair throughout his childhood, would the legs atrophy? It
seems likely that imagination does atrophy if a child grows de-

pendent on pre-made images in the form of television, music videos and video games. I have no proof to offer, but can refer you to a study that suggests that people feel passive and less alert after watching television.[9] At any rate, whether it is television, or technology in general, or some unidentified culprit, does not really matter, what does matter is that something seems to be having a deadening impact on imaginations. Let me quote the storyteller Marni Gillard, who tells why and how she switched from teacher to storyteller:

> When I taught undergraduate and graduate students in education for a few years, I saw the extent to which teaching conformity has deadened the minds of students. I was shocked to see men and women preparing to be teachers become furious that I, their professor, wouldn't tell them flat out what to learn. They wanted to be able to go home and learn only that (whatever "that" was) so they would be prepared to spit "it" back on a test "covering" only what I had promised the test would cover. Those students had let their ability to think and question and learn independently atrophy. . . . School to them had become a matter of being told what to learn and being rewarded with a good grade for learning it. I was discouraged to think people with that attitude would become the next generation of teachers.
>
> . . . I had to do my best to feed the flame of learning now dim within them. If I criticized them I would just perpetuate the problem . . .[10]

It is not only to visualize stories for entertainment that we need imagination; it is needed in all of life. Those of the persuasion that rational thinking is all-important need to be reminded that even Einstein declared that, for a scientist, *imagination is more important than knowledge.*

The thesis of *The Dream Society*, a recent book by futurist Rolf Jensen, is that the age of information is going to last only another ten or twenty years at the most, and what will follow will be an age in which information will be handled almost entirely by machines, just as hard physical labor is now, and what will be prized in the corporate world will be the ability to imagine.

And yet almost all of public school education is aimed at training a child to develop rational thinking rather than creative, intuitive thinking. Maybe that was all right in a day when a child's play stimulated creativity with imaginary games, but now much of that play is passive in nature, and imagination needs to be valued by and developed by schools, just as much as logical thinking.

Nor is it just the corporate world and entertainment that need an active imagination. Daily life needs it as well, for the ability to envision consequences and thus make ethical decisions and resist peer pressure and for the ability to cope with change or to grow spiritually. This makes the development of imagination important to not only the individual but also to society as a whole.

So, here is where the two parts of the title, the work and the play, join and overlap. I believe that our approach to helping children become readers is too rational, both in method and intent. Developing the skill to read textbooks and business reports will not be enough. In order for it to *work*, the process must become *play*. In order for it to become meaningful, the search cannot be only analytical. Whole language is a good idea, but children's minds must be allowed to breathe, naturally, and should not be forced into seeing literature as question-and-report fodder in history or English or social studies.

The poet and novelist Naomi Shihab Nye says,

> I think young readers have a keen desire to participate in what they read, as opposed to just standing back and admiring, or commenting on a poem from a distance. This is what can be wrong with the dull analysis that too often goes on in classrooms: people try to talk about the poems rationally, logically, literally, taking them apart without ever putting them back together again, or considering them in their wholeness again—which implicitly abandons the wonderment, the exquisite magic at the core . . .

Young readers truly want and need to be involved—they yearn
for poems to touch and move them, to make a deeper "sense"
than explanation does, and to help kindle thought of their own
experiences, reaffirming their lives, offering connections,
links, validations.[11]

How does discovering this meaning become play, then? My
answer is in story listening. Whether it is listening to books read
aloud or to traditional told stories or to the recounting of family
stories does not matter. What matters is the hearing of tales in an
emotionally nourishing setting that allows the mind to relax and
develop the skills of imagination; this is not the time to be working on critical thinking skills of analysis in preparation for questions at the end. We trust children's digestive systems to absorb
nutrition, why not trust their brains to digest ideas?

Birkerts, again, had a considerable amount to say about this
act of listening to stories:

> Being read to is, more than any later reading engagement can
> be, a complete environmental experience—story being read
> cannot always be separated out from the circumstance of its
> presentation. The parent or guardian in close—safe-making
> physical proximity; the child is the focus of all attention; the
> story is served up with all the nuances of inflection, is spun in
> a personalized way toward the listener . . .

> . . . What the reader . . . discovers—and the nonreader may
> remain forever oblivious of—are the dynamics of private
> imagination, how it is that a certain pressure of attention and
> self-investment produces—independent of absolutely every-
> thing else in the reader's life—the sensation of a world. There
> is something that feels vitally self-empowering about running
> the eyes along rows of print and having rise up and then stay
> fixed a whole order of what seems like reality.

> . . . Creating a world fully fledged from markers on a page is
> an attainment that feeds the growing child's sense of self in
> ways we cannot begin to guess at. I would go further: no
> amount of compensatory feel-good activity can compensate

for the loss of this primary sense of agency. It throws wide the doors to inwardness and nothing could be more important.[12]

. . . By the same token, a complete lack of this aptitude, or sense, leaves the individual strangely—and sadly—marooned in the here and now, less able to gain all the different degrees of reflective distance (and detachment) that enable a more sophisticated and, possibly, empathetic "reading" of a given situation. Nonreaders are all too apt to become literalists, individuals challenged by a lack of comparative perspectives in situations . . .[13]

This is the strength reading has to offer. A reader can learn about situations without having to live them. I like to think of it as a kind of "rehearsal" for reality. It provides the luxury of considering possible responses and their probable results in a way practical life seldom offers. Aristotle discussed the cathartic effect of theatre; reading also offers privacy and time and the advantage of imagining ones own visual version of the characters and plot.

Simply learning to listen is another issue that needs consideration. Listening pervades all our life, not just story. We all seek to communicate and to both understand others and be understood by them, and listening is, after all, our chief means of gaining that understanding. Listening, like reading, is deeper than is first apparent. It requires effort as opposed to passive hearing. As an educational psychologist put it: "Hearing is a psychological, passive activity; listening is an active, cognitive process."[14] Others have put it this way: Hearing is not really reception of ideas, but, rather, mere bounding sound waves off the eardrum's of those to whom we address our speaking. Listening transcends hearing (sensing sound waves); it involves both sensing and thinking.[15]

In other words, it is crucial for us to learn how to listen. Communication is not possible without it, and far too many of us, with the bombardment of noise has taught most of us to tune sounds out. The old saying "there is none so deaf as he who would not hear," has much truth in it. The trouble is that we have learned how to do this automatically, so that we are not even aware that it is happening. Adults recognize in the middle of committee meetings that they have let their minds wander, and children don't even hear what they consider annoying or "nagging." Most of us now expect to read or write with at least one background noise, music or television, usually, and silence is a rare luxury.

We need to learn to listen attentively, whether to friends, teachers, clients or bosses. It is much easier to learn in childhood, and while experiencing an activity that is pleasurable. That choice of word, *activity*, was deliberate, for the exercising of imagination and thought is an important aspect of the experience of listening. And those activities are not passive; they require effort, even though it is intellectual rather than muscular. Again, this is about choosing to develop abilities in forms of play, rather than in work. It is my belief that such abilities grow better under relaxed and pleasurable conditions.

This is what makes storytelling so valuable. Storytelling offers all the values of reading and those of listening, plus the benefit of being a communal activity, which adds emotional content to the intellectual content. Storytelling is my first choice, but the reality is that becoming a good teller is labor intensive, and in the absence of a good teller, listening to stories read aloud from books has considerable, if not equivalent, value.

It is also good to share books aloud with children, to help them build the sense of the story worlds that are open to all through literacy. I think that this is a major factor in what has been demonstrated as the importance of parents' and other adults' reading to children. It provides companionship as it introduces children to the intellectual community that admits all people and all views into the abstract world of print, in which ideas can be considered and incorporated into one's own belief system—or not—in a setting where there is no punishment for not getting the "right" answer and the reward lies in expanding one's horizons and clarifying one's own thinking and beliefs.

Another reason I push reading aloud is that I fear that children are less and less often *hearing* the formal language of written discourse, so that when they do meet it in a book, their inner ear is unable to hear it. Cinema used to copy the legitimate theatre and its literary language, but that's changed and television consciously chooses vernacular language, and the lowest common denominator of that, to make it seem like the real world. This is true not just in sitcoms and talk shows, but even in dramatic presentations, and as this has become the norm, movies and even live theater have followed the lead. Whether one welcomes this as democratizing theater or regrets it as an effect of show "business," fewer words are being heard, and more "like, you know" fillers are being used.

The upshot of this cultural shift is that, today, only the child lucky enough to come from a family that uses a large vocabulary in ordinary speech or lucky enough to hear literary materials read out loud gets to feel at home in the language of the mind. The democratic ideal is being lost in the appeal to mass appetites. Please don't hear this as snobbery, for that is the opposite of my intent. To begin with, I happily admit to my own enjoyment of movies and sitcoms; my complaint is that few children ever get exposed to anything else—how then can they be expected to develop a taste for anything else? Nor is it a matter of class. Many children come from homes of material wealth but impoverished language just as many come from families rich in imagination but with little money. My point is that *each* child should be introduced to language of the mind. Whether or not he or she later adopts it is irrelevant, *all* children deserve the opportunity to choose.

Reading aloud is something almost every parent and teacher can do, but beyond that, my plea is for the age old art of storytelling, for it is an established means of successfully and pleasurably introducing children to their imaginations. Just as playing and running is better introduction to exercise than army calisthenics, so too, listening to stories for pleasure is better than reading to prepare for tests, if your aim is to be a full person, rather than a successful test taker. Storytelling also introduces the concept of human-scale performance. Storytelling lets young people see that "professional" need not mean technologically enhanced, and that performance need not be glitzy to be interesting. The idea could even expand to encourage children to play the piano or guitar without having a complete band and light show, even though popular culture discourages such activity as "amateur" and "boring."

My concern runs even deeper. Fewer and fewer children are comfortable holding a conversation about anything beyond their daily concerns. How can we be surprised that they find it hard to write when they have not learned to express their thoughts in speech, let alone in formal language? Writing is not just an extension of reading. Reading is an extension of the active skill of listening and writing is an extension of the even more active skill of speech. Children need to talk and tell, as well as hear and listen.

I encourage you to take the time to really talk with your children and tell them the stories from their own heritage. Don't let them know only commercial popular culture. Don't let them grow up to say "I have no heritage," as more than one child has said. Every family has stories—it is important for children to know where their families came from and why ancestors came to America. If you don't know details, there are plenty of stories about life in the United States, stories we all share, regardless of ethnic background. Most Americans now have ancestors from many backgrounds—so there is much to choose from, and, anyway, it is important not just to look in the mirror, but look at our neighbors and friends. One of the best things about America is that there is such a mixture that we can all share some heritages. Being American means we can all eat curry, pizza, hot dogs, fish and chips, and tacos, so why not taste stories from many backgrounds?

It is equally important to hear about everyday things, too, like the silly thing that happened on the day that your mother started fourth grade, or how parents met. Let children tell to you, too. Or, better yet, tell stories they took part in—about when the family took a trip or when a pet was lost and returned by a kind neighbor. Let them think in terms of narrative and of themselves as characters worth telling stories about. This may sound simple, but remember that the National Assessment of Educational Progress (NAEP) said that in 1998 only 23 percent of fourth graders could write an acceptable story.[16] It takes practice to tell or write a decent story.

Also, if you can, take them to hear real storytellers. Clearly there must be a reason that storytelling, and even many stories have lasted from millennium to millennium. There are not many aspects of human cultural history to have survived this way and they are worth honoring until we understand why they have been important so long.

There are social consequences to our lessening person-to-person communication skills, also. John Locke, in his *Why We Don't Talk to Each Other Anymore: The De-Voicing of Society*,[17] says that we are becoming less and less trusting of each other as we communicate more and more through technological devices and less and less in person, face-to-face. It has been said that the non-verbal communication of facial expression, vocal tone and such convey the vast majority of the information in a face-to-face conversation, while the words are much less important. Written language developed many patterns of punctuation to compensate for not having body language, attempting to silently convey pause and emphasis, but most of those patterns are used less and less often now. (When, for example, was the last time you saw a semicolon in an e-mail message?) To "reach out and touch someone" over the phone really works only when the relationship is so based on memory of physical appearance that those expressions can be imagined, and even then it makes the caller long to be there in person.

This brings us back to the quotation from Guy Debord with which we opened:

> It is hardly surprising that children should enthusiastically start their education at an early age with the Absolute Knowledge of computer science, while they are unable to read; for reading demands making judgments at every line. . . . Conversation is

almost dead, and soon so too will be those who knew how to speak.

We do not need to succumb to the fate seen by iconoclastic philosophers, but we do need to heed their warnings. The proper work of childhood is play, and story provides internal play and food for the child's own imagination, and fodder for imaginative physical play. Let us talk to our children, to give them generous vocabularies and give them the option of rooting their thinking in great thoughts. Let us also tell them stories that are metaphors, to give wings to their hearts and imagination.

Notes

1. Guy Debord, *Comments on the Society of the Spectacle*. Trans. by Malcolm Imrie (London: Verso, 1990). Chapter 10 www.notbored.org/commentaires.html (5 April 2002).

2. Wolfgang Iser, *The Act of Reading: A Theory of Response* (Baltimore, Md.: Johns Hopkins University Press, 1978).

3. George Orwell, *Animal Farm* (New York: Harcourt, Brace, 1946).

4. Personal stories are included with the permission of the person to whom they happened.

5. This is attributed to Voltaire by several internet sites, but without a source. Another translation that appears frequently is: *The instruction we find in books is like fire. We fetch it from our neighbours, kindle it at home, communicate it to others, and it becomes the property of all.*

6. Orson Scott Card, Introduction, *Ender's Game*. rev. ed. (New York: Tor, 1991 [1977]).

7. Morton Vildgaas is quoted by Sven Birkerts in "The Secret Life of Children," *School Library Journal* 45 no. 9 (September 1999), 141-143.

8. Sven Birkerts, "The Secret Life of Children," *School Library Journal* 45, no. 9 (September 1999), 141-143.

9. Robert Putnam, *Bowling Alone: The Collapse and Revival of American Community,* (New York: Touchstone, 2000). Putnam attributes this to Kubey and Csikszentmihalyi, *Television and the Quality of Life.*

10. Marni Gillard, *Storyteller, Storyteacher* (York, Me.: Stenhouse, 1996), 175.

11. Megan Schliesman, "Talking with . . . Naomi Shihab Nye: People! People! My Heart Cried Out," *Book Links* 7 no. 6 (July 1998), 40.

12. Sven Birkerts, "The Secret Life of Children," 141.

13. Sven Birkerts, "The Secret Life of Children," 141.

14. Kenneth C. Petress, "Listening: a Vital Skill." *Journal of Instructional Psychology* 26, no. 14 (1999), 261.

15. George T. Vardaman and Patricia B. Vardaman, *Communication in Modern Organizations* (Malabar, Fla.: Robert E. Krieger, 1982).

16. According to the U.S. Department of Education, the NAEP's 1998 results were quite disappointing. The test gave them a few starting ideas and then twenty-five minutes to write a story. The rates of acceptable work were: Grade four 23 percent met or exceeded expectations for their grade, while at Grade eight it was 27 percent and at grade twelve it was 22 percent.

17. John Locke, *Why We Don't Talk to Each Other Anymore: The De-Voicing of Society* (New York: Touchstone, 1998).

Chapter 5

Imagining Information

Introduction to the Talk

This was originally delivered as a Doctoral Colloquium in the Information Studies program of the Palmer School of Library and Information Science, Long Island University. Brookville, New York February 10, 2000.

This was an informal colloquium addressed primarily to doctoral students who were curious about my interest in storytelling.

The fact that several students were looking at the topic of visual information had started me thinking about "envisioning" material and the role of imagination in both telling and listening to stories. The concern for imagination expressed in this lecture also provided the impetus behind a research project concerning imagination, illustration and storytelling, on which I am currently working.

Imagining Information

You, who are the father of letters, have been led by your
affection to ascribe to them a power the opposite of that
which they really possess. For this invention will pro-
duce forgetfulness in the minds of those who learn to use
it, because they will not practice their memory. Their
trust in writing, produced by external characters which
are no part of themselves, will discourage the use of
their own memory within them. You have invented an
elixir not of memory, but of reminding; and you offer
your pupils the appearance of wisdom, not true wisdom,
for they will read many things without instruction and
will therefore seem to know many things, when they are
for the most part ignorant and hard to get along with,
since they are not wise, but only appear wise.

Plato [1]

Reading and writing are things we take so for granted, that it's
hard to remember that they did not always exist, and that when
they came into being they changed forever the way we think. It
was more than two thousand years ago that Plato considered the
impact of writing on humankind and wrote this speech in the
voice of a god talking to the inventor of writing. This criticism of
what we now take for granted is once again relevant, as we turn
other parts of our thinking over to machines. It is time to reconsider Plato's lesson and ask what we risk giving up, and then ask
what can be done to ameliorate the loss and hold on to what is
valuable.

Walter Ong believes that simply knowing that writing exists
changes the way we think so profoundly that it is impossible for
us to understand an oral culture from a modern literate culture.[2]
It is impossible for us to even imagine a true oral culture. Consider the Amish people of Pennsylvania, who live without elec-
tricity or cars, but who are certainly aware of them. Anyone who
has driven a car where horse and buggy traffic share the road can
vouch for the fact that those buggy drivers are very much aware

of the automobile traffic around them. Similarly, cultures that are still oral are affected by their awareness of literate cultures. In other words, we still have a few preliterate cultures in the world, but no longer any that still believe that the spoken word is the only form of language. Few still believe, therefore, that important words are precious enough to memorize exactly and maintain word for word from generation to generation. It was thus that the "books" of the Bible first kept as was the bardic heritage of the Celts and Nordic peoples.

We have not lost the potential for memorizing. Children still can learn songs and stories easily, but not many develop the ability. A few Shakespearean actors can still remember whole plays, and a friend of mine from Iceland can recite eddas for hours. Since this man is a scholar and has read as much as anyone I know, he is a clear example that one can have both memory and reading. Few of us do, however, and the first verse of a few songs is about as much as most of us can manage now. We have let one of our strongest faculties deteriorate. Rote memorization is scorned as a means of learning only of value in "backward" cultures that cannot afford textbooks that hold "real" knowledge. Only now are we beginning to understand that it is not that simple.

The deeper issue is not the aptitude for recitation versus literacy; however, it is that of taking the material into the person. *Knowing* is more than just being able to recall facts; it is being able to make sense of them. It is not just possessing information as a commodity, but making it a part of oneself, letting the knowledge *inform* one's thinking. Plato's concern makes even more sense now as we are being drowned in data and in his words "seem to know many things, when they [we] are for the most part ignorant and hard to get along with, since they [we] are not wise, but only appear wise." Actually, wisdom is not even something many people aspire to any more; being knowledgeable is the goal—or being smart.

Something of this can perhaps be best understood by comparing it with a parallel issue in current awareness. Children's obesity is becoming almost an epidemic. With our technology for moving bodies over long distances without physical effort, and with our technologies for entertainment and education that discourage moving around, we have become very sedentary, and children are paying a price in physical health as a by-product of school buses replacing walking and video games replacing kick the can. It's not primarily the weight that is concerning me, but the lack of exercise and the consequent lessening in strength, grace, skill, and flexibility in motion. Riding a bicycle not only gets the rider to a destination but also develops balance and strength on the way. Walking a country road may be slow, but the walker can hear the birds and see the wildlife and smell the wildflowers, and be a part of that landscape for a while, which is quite different from the tourist passing by and looking from behind a car window. Efficiency has become our primary value and much has been lost that is not even recognized as having had value.

Our new electronic technology has introduced three issues that disturb me. First is the relative value we give to various forms of thinking; we seem to be excessively concerned with what can be handled rationally as data. More abstract pondering is considered irrelevant, or "woolly minded," because it is rarely provable, and our science-based value system wants at least the possibility of proof for its hypotheses before it will even consider them as worth study.

This attitude is beginning to be challenged, however, even in the scholarly community, as we have come to accept that there are issues too ambiguous to be nailed down to single answers. This is evidenced by Emery Roe's *Narrative Policy Analysis*:[3] A brief quote should offer some elucidation:

> What, though, are policy narratives? The short answer is that for our purposes policy narratives are stories (scenarios and arguments) which underwrite and stabilize the assumptions for policymaking in situations that persist with many unknowns, a high degree of interdependence, and little, if any, agreement.

So, narrative and other nebulous forms of communicating are being reconsidered for their "usefulness." Read *Hamlet's Mill: An Essay Investigating the Origins of Human Knowledge and Its Transmission Through Myth,*[4] written by Giorgio de San-tillana, author of *The Origins of Scientific Thought*. The tone is rather apologetic as he discusses how "scientific" information had been transferred from generation to generation by story in the ages before writing was standard and then pays honor to the learning that we lost by discounting myth.

Even current information science is beginning to look at its own roots and see the irony in its own foundings. As Ronald Day says, in discussing the conduit metaphor used by Norbert Wiener in his seminal, *The Human Use of Human Beings: Cybernetics and Society:*[5]

> What is at stake, here, is the question of what authority can make a metaphor not a metaphor, and more generally, what authority can make language not language, but rather, a certain sense of "information" and "communication."

> This is important. Further, however, this issue can then be turned back upon the texts in question, and we can ask what authority can grant that the claims that Weaver and Wiener make in their texts originate in science and not in literature. Throughout *The Human Use of Human Beings*, Wiener re-peatedly appeals to the authority of what he calls "the scien-tist" for what he calls "faith" in science, its techniques, and apparently, its tropes. But this appeal is circular: faith in sci-ence rests upon the authority of science, but this authority it-self rests upon a faith in it.

> . . . These latter claims are political, cultural, and social, and they are based on metaphor, and paradoxically, on a certain faith that this metaphor is not a metaphor, but instead, is an authorizing mark for science.

> . . . information science then provides a somewhat ironically useful function of social self-validation (and for the informa-tion profession, professional self-legitimation). [6]

Before getting tangled up in such ponderings, however, let us continue to a second set of concerns: the content of our new media, who controls this content, and how that affects our society. We are beginning to recognize that what we take in, emotionally and in terms of information, affects us. Just as proper nutrition involves more than sufficient caloric intake, and requires attention to vitamins and minerals, what we spend time thinking about, whether as entertainment or work, does more than just fill up our time, but also has an impact on our personalities. "We are what we eat" is also true of what we think. Schiller, in his *Information Inequality*,[7] worries about how the corporate world has taken over culture, including publishing, and fears that this will result in the blocking of ideas that criticize the status quo. Neil Postman, in his *Amusing Ourselves to Death*,[8] talks about the content and style of television and its impact on education, which now must compete with edutainment. George Gerbner, someone concerned about the violent content of television, says:

> Whoever tells most of the stories to most of the people most of the time has effectively assumed the cultural role of parent and school, teaching us most of what we know in common about life and society. In fact, by the time children reach school age, they will have spent more hours in front of the television than they will ever spend in college classrooms. Television, in short, has become a cultural force equaled in history only by organized religion. Only religion has had this power to transmit the same messages about reality to every social group, creating a common culture. [9]

Nigerian-born writer Ben Okri puts it rather succinctly:

> To poison a nation, poison its stories. A demoralised nation tells demoralised stories to itself. Beware of the storytellers who are not fully conscious of the importance of their gifts, and who are irresponsible in the application of their art: they could unwittingly help along the psychic destruction of their people.[10]

One can argue about the value of what is prevalent today, but few would argue that there is no impact. So, assuming agreement on these two issues, the overwhelming emphasis on logical rather than narrative thinking, and the predominance of commercially produced, consumer-oriented culture over home-made original arts and games, it is time to introduce a third even more basic point upon which we need to focus. Not just *which styles* of thought we value, or *what* we think about, but the very *way* we think, the *how* of it. In line with Plato's "bottom line" of losing the ability to take things through the ear into the memory and thus into the heart, is the question of how newer media affect the very *way* we think and think things up; in other words, our ability to visualize.

It is a matter of the extent to which we risk losing the ability to imagine. Even those who enshrine reason need to take note. Imagination appears to be the basis of creativity, and of empathy. Not only must one have it to be able to imagine how another might feel, and, thus, develop a sense of compassion and justice, but also to be able to create new forms. In other words, it is not just "niceness" and "aesthetic feeling," that are being threatened—the very "efficiency" that has been so scornful of story needs imagination to thrive.

The current model of the human mind as a computer falls short because it emphasizes rationality but leads to ignoring the ability to originate ideas. Now we paint by numbers and fantasize within the limits of pre-packaged games. We call imagining "imagineering"[11] and limit it to predetermined purposeful ends. This is not enough. As the phrase goes, it is an infinite distance from zero to one and a short distance from one to two. We need people who can go that zero to one distance with a new idea much more than people who can take a concept from version 1.5 to 1.6.

It is not just those interested in storytelling and other arts programs who express concern over the lack of ability with imaginative expression. Someone who provides programs for parks and other institutions says that there has been a noticeable decrease over the last twenty years in children's ability to initiate imaginative games and that there is much more reliance on adults to make the first move and support the game.[12] If humankind is becoming dependent on direction even in childhood play, it is losing much of its flexibility.

Nor is it only those concerned with children who see a change. According to one television reporter, Americans have become almost inarticulate, while people from the third world still think in terms of narrative and have kept the ability to communicate ideas and experience, in spite of lower education levels.[13] Whether or not presenting entertaining news shows seems a priority, the implications are quite powerful. Narrative has been a means of sharing information, experience and ideas throughout human history, and if technologized man is losing the ability to tell coherent stories, it is of great significance and should be of real concern.

Part of the issue is the ability to think and express things narratively and part of it is the ability to imagine. What does "imagination" really mean? Listen to author Ursula Le Guin,

> . . . By "imagination," then, I personally mean the free play of the mind, both intellectual and sensory. By "play" I mean recreation, re-creation, the recombination of what is known into what is new. By "free" I mean that the action is done without an immediate object of profit—spontaneously. That does not mean, however, that there may not be a purpose behind the free play of the mind, a goal; and the goal may be a very serious object indeed. Children's imaginative play is clearly practicing at the acts and emotions of adulthood; a child who did not play would not become mature. As for the free play of an adult mind, its result may be *War and Peace,* or the theory of relativity.

> To be free, after all, is not to be undisciplined. I should say that the discipline of the imagination may in fact be the essential method or technique of both art and science . . . in the proper sense of the word . . . to train it—to encourage it to grow, and act, and be fruitful, whether it is a peach tree or a human mind.[14]

Le Guin was writing back in the 1970s when she was concerned with what she saw as Americans' apparent fear of fantasy and fantasizing, but the situation has only become more drastic. Although science fantasy is fairly common video fare, the situation regarding personal imaginations has worsened. Since the advent of television, people who care about reading have been sounding alarms about the huge numbers of us who have almost completely replaced fiction reading with television watching. Now, the internet is taking on the role of provider of non-fiction and completes the shift to pre-prepared visuals from solid print. At least there is no question that the appetite for story and information continues, regardless of format. Now, fiction demand is met by film, and informational demands more often are met in image as well. This is true not just with television news, but also in heavily illustrated books and magazines and on many websites.

So what? So, wonderful new media have come into being for the expression and communication of ideas, but they mean depending more heavily on externally produced visuals, and people are less and less comfortable thinking up their own. People now read books *after* viewing the film—so they can know in advance what the people and places look like. The problem lies not in the new media but in human inertia which has in large part invited those media to take over, so that imagining is becoming the work of professionals to be enjoyed by lay admirers. This is just what the French philosopher Guy Debord predicted in his *Society of the Spectacle.*[15] And this is happening at a time when many futurists[16] predict that imagination workers will soon be in even higher demand than information workers have been.

Think about what is happening to imagination as society becomes more and more accustomed to having images presented ready-made. This is directly parallel to Plato's concern. Not only do computers give us electronic ways to replace memory, which is an extension of the writing Plato discussed, but, more crucially, things are being, literally, visualized for people, and fewer and fewer of us are comfortable imagining for ourselves. *Memory gave us personal links to the past; visualizing is needed to give us links to the future.*

One proven way of developing the ability to imagine is by listening and by reading. What matters is not the logical decoding, but the visualization one must do to "flesh-out" in the mind's eye what the words said. This can then support other creative endeavors. Imagining is a skill that one can develop easily as a young child, when the brain is open to so much, but it becomes much harder to learn later. Just as with learning languages, another means of learning alternative ways of thinking, it is easier for children than adults. Listening to stories, told or read, exercises the imagination and offers the future-adult access to worlds untold, but worth the telling, if only to oneself. That ability to imagine could be at risk.

Consider that favorite field, picture books. It must be said that picture books have great value in expanding the child's repertoire of styles and images and in making the role of books and stories pleasurable. They also may stimulate visual thinking by introducing new ways of imaging: paralleling the way print introduced new ways of thinking, although fears were once expressed that people who read would no longer think for themselves. What follows, therefore, should not be heard as a condemnation of picture books but as a recognition of the fact that there are costs as well as benefits.

First, and most obvious, is the fact that the child does not create internal images when exposed to a picture book, which means that the imagination is not exercised as it would be with an un-pictured story. Second, someone else's pictures, delightful as they may be, are being taken in instead of the child's own, so that the brain is not full of original pictures but of borrowed images. Third, and perhaps not so obvious, the standard of published picture is far above that of the child's own ability and could convince the child that his own picture drawing and imagining abilities are not worth pursuing. I remember very clearly the moment when I gave up on art. I was seven and could not draw a perfect circle even though I tried very hard. Others of my classmates could, which convinced me that I was a failure as an artist, although until that moment I had loved to draw. Think of what the current child, saturated with video images, must think of his or her own artistic ability in comparison.

Current culture has elaborate mechanical gyms to compensate for the fact that machines have replaced human physical labor. Even the effort of playing has been pre-empted by commercial sports. What will society produce to compensate for the lack of original imaginative activity? Will it all be vicarious virtual reality with pre-planned and pre-imaged limits? Will all fantasy be manufactured and run by programmers or dungeon masters running on-line games? Will only James Bond have any fun?

Education is already feeling the results of the dying out of individual imagination, and not just in terms of artistic creativity. One educator has said that students have "let their ability to think and question and learn independently atrophy."[17] She was concerned about formal education, when those students become teachers, but the issue is really society wide.

The impact is particularly clear, already, in terms of what is acceptable in ordinary language. I worry about how we teach reading—not the methods, but the attitudes to it. Those of us in the academy, who have learned to be comfortable with print, take reading for granted, but it is a very complex process, and fewer people are becoming fluent readers, comfortable with the complex literatures of the past. The very word-processing program on which this is being written presents a case in point. Much of the vocabulary is not recognized, and a sentence more than twenty words long is "wrong" according to the grammar checker. So much for the compound sentences and complex thoughts of the not-so-distant past.

In our pop-culture media world, only a few children are exposed to an extensive vocabulary. We are splitting into a small literate elite and a large semi-literate but a-literate world which happily eschews the world of books. I use the word *elite*, because I think those with large vocabularies to use at work and play are better off, but, as it stands, such people risk being resented as "snobs" or brushed aside as eccentrics by "normal" people. At any rate, popular culture has clearly taken over as the norm, and vocabularies are shrinking. Since thinking is done primarily with words, that may well mean that our ingredients for thoughts are also shrinking.

Film used to copy theater, which was a literary tradition, but television has taken over, with its desire to hold up a mirror to everyday life and be accessible to the lowest common denominator, so it uses only the most ordinary of words. This is what children (along with the rest of us) are exposed to. Even the children of the wealthy and educated spend most of their waking hours with television or in day care, and rarely get to listen to, let alone participate in, serious conversations discussing important issues, as we once did around the dinner table or in high school debating societies. It is harder to become literate than it used to be, and competition comes from some very seductive, even addictive, media. Formal literary language has become a foreign language to most Americans.

To get back to the basic idea, though, as we have become dependent on prepared images our "*image-inations*" have suffered. Many children now, literally, find it hard to read because they find it hard to transfer the decoded words into images and, thus, into understanding. Presenting images makes those immediate words easier to understand, but does not exercise the ability to envision one's own images. Film can offer us the chance to enjoy a plot and empathize with characters, but it does not ask us to form our own images, and may not allow us to put our own subconscious material into it in the same way as with un-shown story.

As Bruno Bettelheim put it:

Like the patients of Hindu medicine men who were asked to contemplate a fairy tale to find a way out of the inner darkness which beclouded their minds, the child, too, should be given the opportunity to slowly make a fairy tale his own by bringing his own associations to and into it.

This, incidentally, is the reason why illustrated storybooks, so much preferred by both modern adults and children, do not serve the child's best needs. The illustrations are distracting rather than helpful. Studies of illustrated primers demonstrate that the pictures divert from the learning process rather than foster it, because the illustrations direct the child's imagination away from how he, on his own, would experience the story. The illustrated story is robbed of much content of personal meaning which it could bring to the child who applied only his own visual associations to the story, instead of those of the illustrator.

> . . . a fairy tale loses much of its personal meaning when its figures and events are given substance not by the child's imagination, but by that of an illustrator. The unique details derived from his own particular life, with which a hearer's mind depicts a story he is told or read, make the story much more of a personal experience. Adults and children alike often prefer the easy way of having somebody else do the hard task of imagining the scene of the story. But if we let an illustrator determine our imagination, it becomes less our own, and the story loses much of its personal significance.

> Asking children, for example, what a monster they have heard about in a story looks like, elicits the widest variations of embodiment: huge human-like figures, animal-like one, others which combine certain human with some animal-like features, etc—and each of these details has great meaning to the person who in his mind's eye created this particular pictorial realization. On the other hand, seeing the monster as painted by the artist in a particular way, conforming to *his* imagination, which is so much more complete as compared to our own vague and shifting image, robs us of this meaning. The idea of the monster may then leave us entirely cold, having nothing of importance to tell us, or may scare us without evoking any deeper meaning beyond anxiety.[18]

Think about the act of creating one's own images. Or, maybe, it is easier to see in the context of another age's toys— think, as a parallel, about whether playing a player piano would enable one to become a pianist, or a composer? With the constant impact of powerful, commercially produced images, how can a child's own images not seem puny second choice even to himself. Does the imagination need active and enthusiastic practice to develop? I suspect so, although I cannot prove it.

The value of new forms is not in question. The advantages of being able to present things easily in table form are obvious, as are those of new software that uses the idea of mind mapping to take advantage of the way we usually think—which is not, to begin with, in the straight lines of measured prose. Such forms make things a lot easier for many people. Our ways of viewing the world have often been enriched by film and photo, just as we were enriched by the novel as a consequence of the printing press. Wonderful new media have been and are being developed with new electronic forms. The problem lies in the fact that our imaginations have been so filled with the images of commercially produced media, that it is a rare person that can think outside them.

I have been dismayed by the many graduate students in storytelling classes who can only learn stories from picture books—they are unable to imagine their own versions from print sources. Even more distressing is that huge numbers of children cannot create illustrations that are not copied. A former student, who is now working for a wealthy private school, has expressed her concern that these pupils, when asked to imagine and tell new stories, can only do so in the context of television shows that they already know. It is not just "underprivileged" children being affected.

The simple answer is that we need to develop ways of supporting the growth of imagination among children. Storytelling is a good answer, listening to told stories and learning to tell them. There is something about the shared activity that offers a compensation for the lack of prepared pictures. Maybe there is a shared unconscious, such as Carl Jung describes, that supports the inexperienced imaginer, but something seems to happen that draws people together and allows each person to find his or her own meaning in a tale, even if it is only a confirmation of the self for "already knowing that." Reading aloud and listening to recorded books may help, also, for they give pronunciation and context for formal literary vocabulary. Storytelling offers all that and more—an interpersonal element that welcomes even the reluctant listener into participation and feeds the hunger for occasions shared in trust and enjoyment.

People, adults and children both, are attracted to story. We have different tastes. Some only want biography or other "factual" tales, others only Bible stories, but all hunger for something —and for good reason. To quote Le Guin, again:

a person who had never listened to nor read a tale or myth or parable or story, would remain ignorant of his own emotional and spiritual heights and depths, would not know quite fully what it is to be human. For the story—from *Rumplestiltskin* to *War and Peace*—is one of the basic tools invented by the mind of man, for the purpose of gaining understanding. *There have been great societies that did not use the wheel, but there have been no societies that did not tell stories.*[19]

There is much more to say, about the importance of imaginative thinking skills, about the importance of story in developing a moral imagination, and much more. The main thing is that we need to develop the abilities that will enable us to think in new and unexpected ways, to see parallels and relationships in which none had existed before, to see things that are not immediately in front of our eyes, and, finally, to become at least dimly aware of the complexities of our own inner selves. Much of this is short-circuited when the imaging has already been done for us.

Little is to be gained by taking on the role of Don Quixote and tilting at electronic windmills. Let us simply use the skills of narrative thinking, to imagine possible outcomes, anticipate side effects, and plan ways to circumvent problems. It is silly to ignore the powerful impact of stories and yield the floor completely to those with commercial interests at stake. It is an ancient truth, but still valid, that, in the words of a Hopi proverb:

The one who tells the stories rules the world.

Notes

1. Plato, *Phaedrus* (Fowler translation). Available at: plato.evansville.edu/texts/fowler/phaedrus14.htm (10 January 2000). Plato was speaking in the role of the Egyptian God-King Thamus, to Theuth, the inventor of writing.

2. Walter J. Ong, *Orality and Literacy: The Technologizing of the Word* (New York: Routledge, 1988 [1982]).

3. Emery Roe, *Narrative Policy Analysis: Theory and Practice* (Durham, N.C.: Duke University Press, 1994).

4. Giorgio de Santillana and Hertha von Dechend, *Hamlet's Mill: An Essay Investigating the Origins of Human Knowledge and Its Transmission Through Myth* (Boston: Godine, 1977 [1969]). Santillana is also the author of *The Origins of Scientific Thought from Anaximander to Proclus, 600 B.C. to 300 A.D.* (Chicago: University of Chicago Press, 1961).

5. Norbert Wiener, *The Human Use of Human Beings: Cybernetics and Society* (Cambridge, Mass.: The Riverside Press, 1950).

6. Ronald E. Day, "The 'Conduit Metaphor' and The Nature and Politics of Information Studies," *Journal of the American Society for Information Science* 51 no. 9, (July 2000) Available on-line at: www.lisp.wayne.edu/~ai2398/wiener.htm (25 September 2002). His article is based on ideas found in: M. J. Reddy "The Conduit Metaphor—A Case of Frame Conflict in Our Language about Language." *Metaphor and Thought*, 2nd ed. Cambridge: (Cambridge University Press, 1993), 164-201.

7. Herbert I. Schiller, *Information Inequality: The Deepening Social Crisis in America* (New York: Routledge, 1996), 8.

8. Neil Postman, *Amusing Ourselves to Death: Public Discourse in the Age of Show Business* (New York: Viking, 1985).

9. George Gerbner, quoted in Scott Stossel, "The Man Who Counts the Killings," *Atlantic Monthly* 279 no. 5 (May 1997), 86-104.

10. Ben Okri, #1, "Aphorisms and Fragments from 'The Joys of Storytelling,' " *Birds of Heaven* (London: Phoenix, 1996).

11. This has become a common word in personal growth and business circles, for example: Michael LeBoeuf Ph.D. *Imagineering: How to Profit from Your Creative Powers* (New York: Berkeley, 1986 [1980]).

12. Suzanne Wright Crain, in conversations May 2002.

13. This came out a discussion with two reporters who happened to sit at a neighboring table in a New York restaurant. He had been on the spot almost immediately after the World Trade Center had collapsed, and had not been able to get any interesting interviews. He claimed that it was not that they were in shock, but that people are losing the ability to tell stories. We spent some time talking about storytelling. He was from Fox News Network. [This section was added after the original speech, and was also mentioned in the chapter on the importance of storytelling, but seemed important to re-introduce in this context].

14. Ursula Le Guin, "Why Are Americans Afraid of Dragons?" *The Language of the Night* (Berkeley, Calif.: University of California Press, 1985 [1979]), 41. [Originally published in: *PNLA Quarterly* 38 (1974]).

15. Guy DeBord, *The Society of the Spectacle* (New York: Black & Red, 1977 [1970]). *La Société du Spectacle* (Paris: Editions Buchet-Chastel, 1967).

16. For example, Rolf Jensen, *The Dream Society. How the Coming Shift from Information to Imagination will Transform Your Business* (New York: McGraw-Hill, 1999).

17. Marni Gillard, *Storyteller Storyteacher* (York, Me.: Stenhouse, 1996), 175.

18. Bruno Bettelheim, *The Uses of Enchantment: The Meaning and Importance of Fairy Tales* (New York: Knopf, 1976), 59-60.

19. Ursula Le Guin, "Prophets and Mirrors: Science Fiction as a Way of Seeing," quoted in *The Language of the Night* (New York: Berkeley, 1985 [1979]), 32. ([Originally published in *The Living Light* 7, no. 3 [Fall 1970]).

Chapter 6

Story Is Deeper Than Action

Introduction to the Talk

This was originally delivered at the Queensborough Public Library, Jamaica, New York, May 2, 2000.

When I began working for the New York Public Library we often went to each other's branches to tell stories, so that those carefully memorized stories would reach children in more than one neighborhood. Things ran at a more human, pace then, and library workers took turns providing coffee and some cookies to share together on their afternoon break. It was a very civilizing and democratizing custom, for everyone, librarian and shelver alike, sat down for tea and conversation. It was very good practice for learning to listen to other people's personal anecdotes and opinions and for learning to tell one's own stories in a way that entertained the hearer. Needless to say, we were not conscious of the connection between such conversation and storytelling at the time.

A fellow children's librarian from those days went on to become the head of children's services for the Queensborough Public Library, and when she read the "Myth in the Age of In-

formation" speech in JOYS, she invited me to speak to her chil-dren's librarians to encourage them to do storytelling.

Earlier talks had started me pondering the role of story and imagination in stimulating thought. First was the idea of the connection between being able to converse and to use words for story and next came thoughts about how comfort with words and stories in general supported fluency in thinking about issues in life.

Story Is Deeper Than Action

I overheard one listener remark to a friend:
"Well, now I know stories aren't just some-
thing you tell or hear—they're something
that happens to you when you tell or hear
them."

Kay Stone [1]

This has been called the "information society," and it is certainly
true that information has taken over our consciousness, and our
culture requires people who can understand written data in print
and electronic form. This means that many groups are pushing
for reading so that schools will produce employable, effective
workers who will add to the country's productivity. There is not,
however, an equal concern for *story*, and even less for traditional
storytelling, and they are at much greater risk than reading and of
enormous importance.

The narrative of theater has taken over for our age, and that
in technologized form. Theater, and its current form, film, are
valid story media, but their form is visual and thus different from
spoken narrative. The experience of the audience is different.
Two things concern me. First, action, largely provided by special
effects, is replacing plot, which needs to be carefully thought
through and constructed so that it is coherent. The two terms
used to be interchangeable, but now they seem to be separating.
Sensation is the goal of action, while the esthetic/emotional satisfaction of seeing cause and effect and the way strands are woven
into a whole is the goal of plot. The first is immediate, the second requires time to play out. The second concern is that technological intermediation works very well for sending a message to
a passive recipient, but true communication is a shared activity
and it needs an active receiver as well as sender. Even the name
"instant messenger" recognizes the difference, suggesting that
these are serial messages, not a shared conversation. We need to
be able to communicate mutually.

Storytelling is truly interactive, for the teller is responding to cues from the audience, whether consciously or not. Not surprisingly, verbal narrative, like conversation, is something that works best live. Many types of verbal narrative exist, including sung ballads and epics. For the issue at hand, however, let's focus on traditional storytelling, reading, and reading aloud. They are all important and they share some values, but they have individual benefits as well.

First let us address reading, because it is basic to the current information society which is so dependent on text still, even as graphic information grows in importance. The reading that we do as children is very important, for the books read in childhood matter. At no other time in our lives are we so impressionable and open. As Grahame Greene put it: "Perhaps it is only in childhood that books have any deep influence on our lives . . ."[2] and "There is always one moment in childhood when the door opens and lets the future in."[3] It is often a book that provides that moment.

Those of us who have read hundreds and thousands of books can dismiss any one book or reading experience, for we have a broad perspective. To a child, on the other hand, each book counts, for even the *act* of reading is new and it all matters. Birkerts waxed rhapsodic on this subject in a recent article in *School Library Journal*. He said:

> Do we [as adults] even remember that sense of there being a world existing on the other side of what is, in effect, a code? One cracks at it, keeps cracking—feeling with a genuine thrill how another reality assembles itself in direct response to one's exertions. What mastery and command derive from this! The child has a very immediate tactile sense of how the letters and the sounds they make coalesce into meaning, a sense that largely disappears as the process becomes more automatic.[4]

That thrill of learning to read is wonderful to behold. I was lucky enough to be visiting a friend while she was taking care of her niece and actually witnessed this child break through from the stage of struggling letter by letter to suddenly recognizing whole words, and fancy ones at that, so that she could glory in the language she was reading aloud to two admiring adults. It was clear from her enjoyment in the sounds that she is a lover of words and will become a reader, but that cannot be counted on for all children.

Reading is being given a lot of attention currently, because it is rightly seen as being at risk just when everyone needs to be able to handle text. The biggest problem, really, is that many people choose to avoid reading. They see it as a chore. This is usually the result of two factors—limited reading skill, which makes the effort involved feel more costly than the reward of the results, and the competing appeal of easier occupations that seem to supply the same rewards—most obviously, watching television.

Birkerts mourns another aspect of the loss of reading in his *Gutenberg Elegies*[5]—the loss of that community of readers who read and discussed serious novels. Such people could form instant bonds with each other upon meeting as they discussed and agreed or disagreed over favorites and their meanings. As someone lucky enough to belong to a formal group that does discuss serious fiction for young people, I can attest to that sense of community, and to the fact that there are still fine novels for young people being written—and read.

Connecting this thought with my own concern about storytelling, it occurs to me that the novel may find itself relegated to childhood, as happened with oral story.[6] The perception may be that only in childhood can one rationalize the spending of large chunks of time on an activity with no immediate visible results; and even then it is justified by the conviction that it is good for children—that it will help them learn to read well and thus do well in school and in getting a job. I think that story is important for adults, as well as for children, to keep healthy, but it is crucial in childhood to develop as a full person. Imagination and empathy must be developed in tune with each other if we want solutions rather than just more effective means of feeding the appetites for power and pleasure. Whether supplied as books or told stories, children need narrative.

It is hard to know what to do to promote reading, and I fear that we have made some terrible mistakes. It's as if the fundamental goal of producing individuals who understand and value the gifts of reading has been lost in the school's need to produce children who can read to pass tests. The consequence of this is that that most children now reject the entire medium of reading, regardless of the message contained in the book, be it textbook, novel, or joke anthology.

As adults we can see that children need encouragement when the excitement of learning to decode those words has worn off, and we hope that just by making sure they practice we can ensure that these children will arrive at the skill level at which they can get lost in a book and become hooked on reading. There is danger, though, in acting as if reading were not its own reward. I even have mixed feelings about library summer reading programs that offer prizes for reading. We don't reward them for playing basketball, why for reading? Is it really as unpleasant a task as carrying out the garbage? There is a message there, whether or not we are conscious of it, and whether or not it is intended. If it is politically necessary to participate in such programs, the prizes should be offered in a sense of shared celebration of reading, rather than as a payoff, and we should not pay "by the book" but simply celebrate what is gained by becoming readers.

In answer to the problem, I would prefer that we simply honor the fact that children's interest outpaces their ability to read, and so read to them and have them read to you, to keep them enthusiastic about books and yearning for further skill. As evident, let me tell you of twins I know. One of them was reluctant to admit that she had learned how to read because she was afraid that it would mean giving up sharing books with her mother at bed-time. It caused problems at school, but her twin sister encouraged her in her deception because, although that twin had been openly reading since they were three, she too wanted to keep the bedtime book sharing.

Far too often, learning to read does mean just such an ending. Reading aloud to children is a means of sharing the pleasure of books, and shared interest in factual topics can be as satisfying as stories. Enthusiasm on the part of a parent or teacher can also introduce new topics that might not otherwise be part of a child's awareness. This not only increases learning but also establishes reading as a desirable occupation that satisfies curiosity. The continuing success of Jim Trelease's *Read-Aloud Hand-book*[7] proves that children's librarians were right all along about the importance of sharing books aloud.

It is not surprising that books recorded on tape or CD are growing enormously in popularity for all ages. Scott Turow has spoken of how much it pleases him to have his books recorded because it creates a full-circle and connects his fiction with traditional storytelling and communicating by voice.[8] Listening to tape is wonderful, particularly when it is the only option, as when commuting in a car, but it is rarely as satisfying as a live reading. It is interesting to see how reading is reappearing in concert form, as with Selected Shorts (a program featuring literary stories read aloud). This is true even for children. A reading aloud from the Harry Potter books at the Brooklyn Academy of Music drew hundreds to sit and listen quietly to a single voice reading and earned tremendous applause.

A friend of mine who grew up long ago in Cuba told me of working in a cigar factory as a child and listening to Dickens being read aloud (in Spanish). She loved it and struggled to learn to read herself so she could do it. Years later, she used her reading to escape poverty, completing high school in her thirties and even going on to medical school. The point here is not her success but that listening was seen as a pleasurable activity that made rolling cigars less boring. Remember that these were not literary, sophisticated people anxious to demonstrate their love of world literature, but simple workers who knew a good story when they heard it.

It is important for literacy development that children be exposed to the vocabulary of formal, literary language. There are innumerable terms and idioms that are rarely used in common household parlance but that are frequently employed in narrative or discursive writing or in formal oration, as exemplified by the circumlocutory verbiage that currently falls upon your captive auditory apparati. If the inner ear is unable to hear these words, it is as if they were a foreign language. It takes years of exposure to written language to become comfortable with *enough* words to be able to tolerate those you are not sure about and must understand only from the context. Few children hear such words in conversation or on the television screen, now, so reading aloud is very important for both pronunciation and comprehension.[9]

In a similar development, writing is following the lead of the spoken word. Think of the difference between e-mail and traditional formal letters. We are losing all of the nuances of carefully chosen words and elaborate punctuation and subordinate clauses that were developed in order to make sure that written messages would be as understandable as face-to-face ones. Now emoticons are being used to reinvent the wheel of written messages, and people are sending e-mail with no words at all.

It takes only a moderately melodramatic point of view to worry over whether our culture is squandering our children's intellectual birthright. Many have predicted a breakdown of society into literate and illiterate or semi-literate classes. Will it be only a very limited number of children who get exposure to the language of great thinkers of the past? My democratic ideals find this frightening. It is not a matter of money but of what we as a society demand for our children. Tastes change, of course, but there are many well-written books that retain their appeal. Elsie Dinsmore is out, but the Little House books still maintain children's interest. It is like nutrition. One could feed children nutritious meals inexpensively enough, with rice and beans and fresh vegetables, but that requires thought, time, and effort, while it is easier and far more appealing to them to provide fast foods and feel "in synch" with the world of commercial popular culture.

Clearly, not every adult will choose a world of thought, but all children deserve the chance to be introduced to it and decide for themselves instead of having the choice made by circumstances that limit exposure to an enriched vocabulary. This goal can be supported by reading aloud, for it provides entertainment, encouragement and enrichment of language. Listening is a learned skill, and one is far more likely to learn how to listen well if one hears material that gets the attention pleasurably, as stories do.

Now we come to the main entry of my plea—storytelling. It is the most basic form of shared imagination of them all, being something that predates reading in both human civilization and in any individual's life. We are all storytellers, every day. From complaining about the disasters that happened on the way to work, whether a delayed subway or stolen parking place, to relating the latest episode of your favorite soap opera or sitcom, to convincing a potential mate of the bliss you could share, we all need to recount sequences of events and convince listeners. What is our legal system but trial by rival stories about the same circumstances?

Story is one of the most common and most powerful forms of human communication. The Nigerian-British writer, Ben Okri, a man raised in both oral and written literature traditions, has said: "Like water, stories are much taken for granted. They are seemingly ordinary and neutral, but are one of humanity's most powerful weapons for good or evil."[10]

Traditional storytelling is a relatively rare event in modern society, however. Still, there is a National Storytelling Festival in Jonesborough, Tennessee, that proves that storytelling is not dead. But there are many changes even there, not the least of which is the shrinking proportion of folk tales, which are being replaced as tastes tend to personal story and popular patter and music shows. All are worthwhile, but I am concerned with the survival of the folk tale tradition.

This tradition was, incidentally, kept alive in children's libraries for many decades while popular culture moved in very different directions. Librarians can be proud of their heritage as storytellers. It was not always easy. At the time I began, many viewed storytelling as embarrassingly "old fashioned," like homemade clothes. At The New York Public Library, librarians were not offered a choice. One either was a storyteller or one was not a children's librarian. That was it. One may or may not have told well, but one told stories. I am grateful for that experience, but I can also remember feeling reluctant about being associated with either the cutesy "kiddie" tellers or over-earnest ones who felt they were going to save the world.

Now, here it is my turn to preach the value of storytelling. At least I am old enough that I don't embarrass that easily anymore and, as the wheel of time has turned, the world is redeveloping an interest in story. Society is beginning to recognize some of the valuable things we lost in the development of our commercial, technological culture. Jensen predicts that computers will soon take over rational tasks and it will be the dreamers and storytellers who will be valued.[11] Assuming there is some basis to his assertion, that means that it is important for children to be exposed to stories early and often, so that imagination will become a normal part of their thinking.

Why do I emphasize stories rather than books? Because, although reading is a skill that can give access to stories, it is the impact of the story that I am concerned with here, and I think that listening to stories is in many ways more valuable than reading. It is a human-to-human direct connection, unlike the abstract world of print or the disembodied voice of the tape. The so-called renaissance in storytelling and the popularity of books on tape attest to the hunger for story-listening, but I am more concerned with the intellectual *nutrition* than with the taste.

A significant element of my concern is that children seem to be finding it harder to imagine than they used to because they are not used to imagining and visualizing from scratch. Even music, the art of sound, now comes as a video, not just an audio. People buy books *after* they see the movie, so they will know what the characters look like. News comes with live footage. Magazines and books are filled with pictures. When children are read bedtime stories they are usually from books with pictures.

Years ago Bettelheim worried about picture books, fearing that children's minds would not make use of the old tales in the way past generations had done. Psychologists some time ago learned that children took the stories into their subconscious minds and used them to resolve internal conflicts. For example, the evil stepmother of so many tales for girls did not represent a literal stepmother so much as the part of the real mother that did not meet the girl's needs and wishes. Here was a way to safely feel anger at cruel mothers in the abstract without having to threaten the relationship with one's own.

The old tales had worked well for millennia, but now there were pictures of the characters and, according to Bettelheim, the child's mind would no longer identify with the characters and do the subconscious work on his or her own relationships, but would instead see the characters as those external people. These books would then provide entertainment but would not help with the job of growing up. I believe that he was overstating it, that the pattern comes into the mind and can be reconfigured as necessary by the subconscious, but it is an interesting idea to consider.

We will come back to this, but the point at hand is about the development of the mind. If images are always supplied, the ability to visualize is going to atrophy. Use it or lose it seems to apply to the mind as well as the muscles. Currently, children have their minds filled primarily with commercially visualized fantasy.

Play has changed. In the past, children would get together and invent games. I remember being very small and watching my big brother and his friends playing Robin Hood in homemade costumes and, a little later, joining my own friends in inventing stories and costumes of our own. A modern child is more likely to have a bought outfit representing a figure from commercial popular culture and less likely to be engaging in impromptu group imaginative play. Children now tend to be in adult-organized activities and do not often have either the casual neighborhood groups or the unsupervised leisure time that produces these spontaneous games. This perception is shared by others who work with children as teachers or in play situations and have perceived a decline in imaginative spontaneity.[12]

Acting out stories is clearly imaginative play, but it is the interior visualization that is important in the current context. For a long time educators assumed that decoding was all that was required for reading, but they are coming to recognize that many people can read the words but still not put them together in a meaningful way. For that, you must be able to visualize. Most librarians are good at this; after all, few would be attracted to this

profession unless reading was easy for them. That makes it hard
for most of us here today to imagine not being able to visualize.
There is an old trick of asking someone not to think of elephants,
which immediately brings elephants to mind. What if you
couldn't visualize—how bleak it would be. You would be dependent on what was presented from outside. Further, you would
not have the option of using books as portals to the worlds of the
mind.

This concern with making visualizations is not limited to book
people. An interesting message that appeared on the Storytell
Listserv a while ago brings a different perspective to the issue.
The writer, who is a filmmaker, was complaining about the fact
that few children have access to video equipment. She believes
that part of the problem of low imagination comes from our being used to passively accepting visual information. As a consequence of this low awareness level, we are less questioning than
is good for society because we do not know how things are
done—which leaves us unable to imagine how things might have
been done. These are valid points.

It is not necessary for us to be as dependent as we are. As a
society we could all be visually literate and also able to create
visually. If that should happen, it would relieve considerable
anxiety about the future, which is clearly already more visual
than the linear print one that used to be the norm.

The issue at hand, though, is not visual sophistication but the
ability to create visualizations from narrative. I want to quote a
bit more from Birkerts:

> What the reader . . . discovers—and the nonreader may remain
> forever oblivious of—are the dynamics of private imagination,
> how it is that a certain pressure of attention and self-
> investment produces—independent of absolutely everything
> else in the reader's life—the sensation of a world. There is
> something that feels vitally self-empowering about running the
> eyes along rows of print and having rise up and then stay fixed
> a whole order of what seems like reality.[13]

This addresses the importance of both the act of reading and the story in developing self-esteem and self-awareness in general. He also says:

> . . . By the same token, a complete lack of this aptitude, or sense, leaves the individual strangely—and sadly—marooned in the here and now. . . . Nonreaders are all too apt to become literalists, individuals challenged by a lack of comparative perspectives in situations.[14]

S.I. Hayakawa said something similar:

> In a real sense, people who have read good literature have lived more than people who cannot or will not read. . . . It is not true that we have only one life to live; if we can read, we can live as many more lives and as many kinds of lives as we wish.[15]

There are two concerns here. Both men are talking about the breadth of experience, secondhand to be sure, but still part of one's thought experience. There is another aspect, though, what I used to call the "vaccination for experience" theory. How much better to meet a situation for the first time in a fictional setting than to have to cope with it in real life, when the stakes are higher. Unfortunately, most of us meet a bogeyman or two along the way. Knowing that you are not the first child to deal with something and that others have survived it and prospered later can help. Slow and steady can win the race. Honesty can be rewarded more highly than cleverness, as in the story of the empty pot. In this story, which is currently very popular, a ruler sets up a contest for the best plant grown from one of the seeds he gives out. As time passes people worry because nothing comes up. Some give up, but many plant a seedling in the pot to take the place of the one that did not sprout. On the day these plants are to be judged, one boy shows up with a pot that has only dirt. The ruler asks why he has no plant like the others, and the sad boy replies that he watered the pot and gave it sun, but nothing came up. The ruler then explains that he had boiled the seeds, to see who had enough honesty and courage to come with an empty pot. The boy is then taken to court, to be trained as the ruler's heir.[16] The story rings true in a way that allows a listener to take the message in; being told that honesty is the best policy can allow the lesson to remain abstract and external.

Now we are getting into the crux of what makes story so important, regardless of the form—what stories do for the hearer. The act of listening to a told story can be a profound experience. It seems to satisfy the subconscious as well as the conscious, including a shared closeness as well as entertainment.

Many stories are just that, entertainment, but others have deeper messages that make a subtle difference in the way we view the world. One of the most common things to happen when telling stories is to have a child ask: "Is that *true*?" They are really asking whether it can be trusted. I find it hard to answer but usually say something like: "Did it really happen? Well, we don't know, but probably not. There is truth in the heart of the story, though. It not like saying 'Yes, I took the piece of cake,' which is a fact but like saying 'I love you' which is also true, but which is based on belief, not fact. It has the truth of wisdom, whether or not it was a fact." Usually, the child nods his or her head in understanding.

I distinctly remember the moment I first saw a "truth" in a book. It was *My Mother Is the Most Beautiful Woman in the World*.[17] This was the retelling of an old Russian tale about a little girl who got lost at the fair, and of all the people who tried to help find her mother, whom she described through her tears as "the most beautiful woman in the world." Needless to say, when momma showed up, she was homely as a mud fence, but beautiful to her Marushka. I remember thinking, "Oh, so that's what they mean by a 'truth.' " Picasso made a lovely comment once. He was talking about the graphic arts, but it works just as well for the kind of storytelling I am talking about. He is supposed to have said: "Art is a lie that tells the truth."

Metaphoric truth is something that we are just beginning to value again, as we face a world of constant change and try to learn how to function within it Ben Okri says: "It is precisely in a broken age that we need mystery and a re-awakened sense of

wonder: need them in order to be whole again."[18] The very un-
certainty of our world requires answers that are flexible. Our
children need to be able to think on their feet. We don't help
them with that very much. We feed them straight factual information and are then surprised when imagination does not develop. We let them be exposed to commercial sellers of dreams,
but give them no experience with imagination to learn how to
judge such material.

The vast majority of our education is aimed at the left half of
the brain, the logical, rational part.[19] It is the right brain that is
the creative, imaginative half. We need both, together as a team.
Bernice McCarthy, an education innovator who developed a way
of learning using both halves of the brain, says:

> All excellence is both [right and left brain]. Listen while the
> master storyteller integrates the language skills of the Left
> Mode with the imaging skills of the Right. She takes the
> linearity of speech and weaves roundness with pictures,
> intonations, dialogues, colors.
>
> Attend the poet who chooses words with the most careful
> precision and forms crystal moments where events hang
> forever suspended as living holograms.
>
> Be with the composer who hears the whole, then in
> painstaking sequence creates the notations which create the
> linearity for the musicians to follow in order to create the
> round he hears.[20]

Let's repeat that idea: ". . . the master storyteller integrates the
language skills of the Left Mode with the imaging skills of the
Right." The story listener, too, connects both language and
imaging skills, both logical and creative thinking. We must
consider both, but for the moment, lets concentrate on the right
half. It is that half that develops ethical behavior and spiritual
ideas. The basis of ethical behavior requires, quite simply, that
the person be able to follow through and visualize the
consequences of his behavior and recognize the impact on
someone else. Empathy needs imagination. The same thing is
true in terms of resisting peer pressure. Long-term goals can win

out over short-term gratifications only if they are visualized internally. Listening to stories not only provides examples, it also develops the ability to figure out one's own.

Perhaps my favorite quote is from Ray Apodaca, an Apache elder who put the difference between left and right brain education very succinctly. He said: *"In the white man's schools, they teach children what to think; we tell them stories and ask them to think for themselves."* [21]

That is it in a nutshell. Today's children must learn to think for themselves, and thinking in terms of story is an excellent training. We are talking about several layers of thinking and meaning here. The first and most obvious is the plot aspect—learning what kinds of consequences follow what kinds of behaviors. There are several moral principles that seem to appear in almost every culture's tales. For example: One must be kind to everyone, even the weak and lowly. You may find yourself in a position of need or of power, but that can change and you can never tell who will turn out to be in a position to affect your life. It may be that the mouse released by the powerful lion will come to that same lion's rescue by gnawing through the ropes that hold him in a trap. It may be that the pathetic woman begging for water turns out to be a powerful being; she may give a kind girl a mouth that spills out pearls and rubies as she speaks but give the cruel sister toads and snakes when she opens her mouth. In the long run, being nice is a better way to live comfortably with yourself, but it also helps to include reminders that virtue is sometimes rewarded externally, as well as being its own reward.

The harsh realities of life are also presented in tales, in bearable form. Sometimes people need to go out to seek their fortune in an unknown outside world. Sometimes people are cruel, even family members. There can be a child unloved by a parent or one who is not respected by brothers and sisters. Sibling rivalry and Oedipal problems existed long before Freud named them. Children are just people and often have painful problems, in spite of our wish that things were otherwise. Being able to respond to story characters' situations can relieve much stress, particularly when they demonstrate that such situations can be resolved, and thus, offer hope for a happy ending.

What coping tactics are offered by example? Well, being nice to others, as we said already. Not only do other people respond appreciatively, but you also like yourself better. And being steadfast is a good idea, since it often takes several tries before a problem is solved. Whether the three times of European tales or the four of Native American tales, patience and perseverance will work to your benefit. Brains can outwit brawn—or can trip themselves up. Finally, keep your heart and eyes open to luck or magic, or hope, and listen to the still small voice inside. Fortune can only win you the lottery if you buy a ticket. The treasure you are looking for may be in your own backyard, but you may have to travel to hear the clues about its whereabouts. All of these themes appear in tale after tale.

None of this is bad advice. Treating others with respect and kindness, using your head, facing fears head-on, working until it's done, and keeping faith and hope through discouragement are all excellent coping strategies for anyone seeking a happy-ever-after ending.

There are many psychologists, who have dealt with myth and fairy tale as means of personal growth. Jung built his whole system on myth, after he came to the conclusion that the same stories and figures appear again and again in human imagination and the archetypes must be part of human emotional make-up. They should, he therefore reasoned, be a key to helping people resolve their neuroses. Likewise, Milton Erickson put together a system for helping people by hypnotizing them and then telling stories tailor-made for their issues. He left the tales open-ended in a way that empowered the hearers to finish them healthily in their own way, and thereby gain strength to deal with the issue in the rest of their lives. Storytelling is also becoming more and more common in therapeutic and alternative healing situations.[22]

Earlier, I mentioned Bettelheim's book *The Uses of Enchantment*.[23] It is a very good introduction to the psychological content and impact of fairy tales. These ideas are still interesting and useful, although Freud is much less fashionable than he was. Another fascinating approach comes in the work of Joseph Campbell and others who look at the mythological systems of the world. One word of caution, though. Although such thinking is fascinating, it can inhibit one as a storyteller. If this material really has such a great impact on the human unconscious, it is strong stuff to be messing around with. I recommend taking a few grains of salt along with this reading, just to keep your sanity.

Freud chose the name "Oedipal Complex" from the Greek story of Oedipus Rex, the king whose father left him to die of exposure when he heard the prophecy that this son would kill him. A passing shepherd saved the boy, who grew up to kill a stranger at a crossroads when he would not let him go first. The young man continued on his journey and married the widow of the slain man. In demanding the truth from the blind seer Teresias, who tried to avoid telling him, Oedipus learns who he really is and then is stuck with knowing the unbearable truth, that he killed his father and married his own mother. This story has remained important for thousands of years, attesting to its appeal to something very deep within us. Freud's idea, as you know, is that every boy wants his mother to himself and must struggle with the mixed feelings he consequently has toward his father.

I do not know whether or not ancient Greeks told this story to their children, but the popular English tale of Jack and the Beanstalk represents a similar childhood issue: that of having to separate from the mother. In this story, Jack and his mother are coming to the end of the time of his dependence, and Jack is told to sell the cow (which symbolizes being weaned from his mother's milk and childhood). He starts to town, but meets a man who offers some magic beans for the cow, and they make the trade. Jack's mother is so angry at his being duped by a con man that she throws the beans out the window and sends him to bed hungry. Lo and behold, in the night, a magic beanstalk grows for him, and Jack climbs it to a magical place where he conquers the giant (who represents powerful, scary fathers), gets away with the giant's fortune, and comes home to confound his mother with his great feats and winnings. It does not require a great deal of adult imagination to recognize a boy's masturbatory fantasies in climbing the beanstalk, which his mother did not recognize as valuable, and understand the thrill of fighting off threatening monsters to return a hero. It is the same issue as Oedipus Rex, in a way, but a much more childlike perspective and a comedy of success rather than the tragedy that Oedipus presents. No wonder boys love it.

I remember a story from my own childhood that I loved, but felt embarrassed by, without understanding why. It was the story of the magic pot, which was given to a little girl by an old lady in the forest and that responded to magic words known only by the little girl, so that the girl's mother got in trouble when she tried to use the pot by herself. I had a very loving mother, but her overwhelming strength sometimes left me feeling weak. As an adult I can see why the story embarrassed me; it was simply too close to my own uncomfortable feelings, so that my conscious self could almost recognize them. Today, of course, this story is best known in the picture book version of *Strega Nona*,[24] which is an amusing mixture of that tale and the sorceror's apprentice. Still, I regret the replacement of the Grimm tale, for it was one of the few that suggested that a little girl might have a power that should be respected.

Max Luthi, writing about the story Rapunzel, said.

> Only with difficulty does one take leave of his old, familiar form of existence; he tends to cling desperately to what he has. He feels that every step forward involves a dying. Every process of development and maturation demands great bravery; to let go, to take leave, requires courage: fear and anxiety can occur.[25]

In discussing this last statement, Francis Uttley said:

> Children to whom we are inclined to be over-protective, show ample courage; to deprive them of tales of violence is to transfer to them our own fears and thus to keep them from facing up to the facts of life. The ancient witch not only represents the wicked establishment, she is also the disordered terror of the adult world.[26]

Does that strike any personal chords? Can you remember the way you felt when you first met the witch in Snow White or the one in *The Wizard of Oz*, or the escaped convict with the hook who attacked teenagers necking in their car? Humans like to release some of their fear onto safe symbols. Hollywood has certainly learned that from folk literature, if nothing else.

Does this mean that I am recommending scaring children? Of course not. Nor was Uttley. We are simply asking that children be respected as people and acknowledged as having a right to develop their inner strength in healthy ways, including facing up to fears and sorrows. Stories have worked their magic for hundreds of generations, and technology has not changed most human needs. Conquering gazillions of robots in the latest video game may feed the same hunger as hero stories, but I suspect they offer less inner nutrition and promote more growth of vanity than of healthy ego.

In our society, we tend to think of storytelling as being something just for children. That, of course, is not really the case. The idea is an historical accident based on the development of literacy and written stories that replaced the told stories that aristocratic and bourgeois European children heard from their illiterate nannies in the nursery. These are the people who grew up to value their later, rational education and in their writing dismiss the peasants and the age-old wisdom of their stories.

Still, it is true that stories are particularly important in childhood. One psychologist who has been working with people trying to design their own mythic systems for psychological and spiritual health, says:

> The fresh and open mind of the child creates and understands myths intuitively, whereas the psychotherapist, the creative writer, and the scholar labor long to mine myth's rich veins of wisdom and creative inspiration.[27]

Our self-conscious age finds formal storytelling difficult, and our education makes the simple story seem too unsophisticated for attention, but it is my belief that it is more important than ever as we face an age in which the very essence of what it means   to   be   human   is   being   redefined.

Notes

1. Kay Stone, "Old Stories/New Listeners," in *Who Says? Essays on Pivotal Issues in Contemporary Storytelling,* edited by Carol L. Birch and Melissa A. Heckler. (Little Rock, Ark.: August House, 1996), 172. Sven Birkerts said something similar, in terms of reading:

> ... there is a very special transformation that takes place when we read fiction that is not experienced in nonfiction. This transformation, or catalyzing action, can be seen to play a vital part in what we might call, grandly, existential self-formation.

Sven Birkerts, *Gutenberg Elegies: The Fate of Reading in an Electronic Age* (New York: Fawcett Columbine, 1994), 91.

2. Graham Greene, *The Lost Childhood and Other Essays* (New York: Lothrop, Lee and Shepard, 1951).

3. Graham Greene, *The Power and the Glory,* (Harmondsworth, England: Penguin, 1940), pt. 1, ch. 1.

4. Birkerts, "The Secret Life of Children," 142.

5. Birkerts, *Gutenberg Elegies.*

6. Birkerts talks about something similar, when he says that literature is becoming less valued because it does not seem to address readers' current lives. *Gutenberg Elegies.*

7. Jim Trelease, *The Read-Aloud Hand-book.* 5th ed. (New York: Penguin, 2001 [1982]).

8. Scott Turow spoke to librarians at a party at the American Library Association annual conference, 14 June 2002, sponsored by Books-on-Tape.

9. Many education researchers have discussed this, notably Jeanne S. Chall, who was concerned with the connection between economic disadvantage and vocabulary and reading skill.

10. Ben Okri, no. 57, "Aphorisms and Fragments from 'The Joys of Storytelling,' " *Birds of Heaven* (London: Phoenix, 1996).

11. Rolf Jensen, *The Dream Society: How the Coming Shift from Information to Imagination will Transform Your Business* (New York: McGraw-Hill, 1999).

12. This comes from many personal conversations with teachers and others.

13. Birkerts, "The Secret Life of Children," 142.

14. Birkerts, "The Secret Life of Children," 141.

15. Samuel Ichiye Hayakawa, *Language in Thought and Action* (New York: Harcourt Brace, 1971), ch. 8.

16. The best-known version is a picture book: Demi, *The Empty Pot* (New York: Holt, 1990).

17. Becky Reyher, *My Mother Is the Most Beautiful Woman in the World*, (New York: Lothrop, Lee & Shepard, 1945).

18. Ben Okri, no. 84, "Aphorisms . . . ", *Birds of Heaven.*

19. The storyteller Elizabeth Ellis told me that she had heard that the figure was 97 percent and that it had come from "On What Works in Education," from the U.S. Department of Education, but I have been unable to find an exact reference through ERIC documents.

20. Bernice McCarthy was quoted in a list of sayings about storytelling that was collected by participants of STORYTELL Listserv. It was originally posted in 1996 by Papa Joe. Her theories are explained in: Bernice McCarthy, *The 4MAT System: Teaching to Learning Styles withRight/Left Mode Techniques* (Wauconda, Ill.: About Learning, Inc., 1987 [1981]).

21. Ray Apodaca, Apache Elder (1992 Native American Symposium held at the Institute of Texan Cultures). (Quoted on Storytell Listserv).

22. There is a special interest group on healing stories within the National Storytelling Association, and some storytellers within the National Expressive Arts Association.

23. Bruno Bettelheim, *The Uses of Enchantment: The Meaning and Importance of Fairy Tales* (New York: Knopf, 1976).

24. Tomie dePaola, *Strega Nona* (Englewood Cliffs, N.J.: Prentice-Hall, 1975). I spoke with him and he confirmed that it was his mixture of the two tales.

25. Max Luthi, *Once Upon a Time: On the Nature of Fairy Tales* (New York: Ungar, 1970), 113.

26. Francis Lee Uttley, introduction, Max Luthi, *Once Upon a Time: On the Nature of Fairy Tale* (New York: Ungar, 1970), 17.

27. Stephen Larsen, introduction, *The Mythic Imagination: The Quest for Meaning Through Personal Mythology* (Rochester Vt.: Inner Traditions, 1996), xvi-xviii.

Chapter 7

Virtual Reality of the Mind: Story

Introduction to the Talk

This was originally delivered as a Doctoral Colloquium in the Information Studies program at the Palmer School of Library and Information Science, Long Island University, Brookville, New York, February 21, 2001

This was another doctoral colloquium. It continued the theme of the importance of listening to stories to help develop imagination and the ability to visualize situations from various points of view. The title grew out of frustration with one student who held that technological virtual reality was an improvement on individual imagination. Ironically, there was a snowstorm on the day it was scheduled, so the student who had prompted it was not present.

Virtual Reality of the Mind: Story

The wayfarer,
Perceiving the pathway to truth,
Was struck with astonishment.
It was thickly grown with weeds.
"Ha!" he said.
"I see that no one has passed here
In a long time."

Later he saw that each weed
Was a singular knife.

"Well" he mumbled at last,
Doubtless there are other roads."

Stephen Crane[1]

There were once two monks who were friends. Both smoked, and they often talked about their smoking. Eventually, each approached the abbot to discuss the issue of smoking and prayer. The first was told that he could not smoke and pray, the other that it was all right. Naturally, the first was upset, and said "I asked the abbot if it was okay to smoke while praying and he told me, 'no.' How did you get permission?" "Ah," said the second, "when I spoke to the abbot, I asked if it were all right to pray while smoking."

This Zen story, obviously set in a very modern Buddhist monastery, always makes me laugh. In spite of its simplicity, a number of things make it worthy of attention. First, it is almost a joke in form, which makes it easy to remember. Second, the situation is instantly understandable. Third, its very simplicity leaves it wide open to interpretation. Is the first monk straightforward and honorable or dull? Is he dismayed, jealous or curious about the different answers? Is the second lucky to have asked the right way or is he deviously clever? Is he smug or surprised by the difference in response? What about the abbot? Was he playing favorites or earnestly trying to dispense wisdom to his flock.

A storyteller can adapt this tale to the occasion and mood of the telling. Think of how it might be used in a business setting, for example. It could be an opener for a discussion on how arbitrary any bureaucracy seems to ordinary staff, or it could begin a discussion on the importance of exactly how issues are introduced to the general public.

In the academic context, on the other hand, it clearly demonstrates the importance of the basic question in a research design. Is it *smoking* or is it *praying* that is the variable?

Except—that is not my point. My point is story, itself, story, as a means of communication. Its very vagueness and ambiguity supplies an amazing flexibility. For generations now, we, as a culture of scientists, have been working on minimizing all vagueness and ambiguity in thought in order to avoid misunderstanding. Now, however, we have so many ways of capturing data permanently in minute detail that accuracy seems ordinary, and concern grows for dealing with nonstandard and complex issues that don't find easy answers in statistical data. That is why such methods as narrative policy analysis are being developed. This approach incorporates varying perspectives and stories to try to provide solutions rather than compromises.[2] The times definitely are changing. Whether or not one agrees with those predicting that the information society is being replaced, there is a noticeable shift in emphasis. People are beginning to notice the forests, as well as the trees.

It was when a researcher from the FindSVP company spent hours interviewing me about storytelling on behalf of a nameless "transnational corporation," that I came to realize that the times they were a-changing. As more and more business books come out like *The Experience Economy: Work is Theatre & Every Business a Stage*[3] and *The Springboard: How Storytelling Ignites Action in Knowledge-Era Organizations*,[4] and as XeroxParc researchers working on the culture of learning tell us that "to make learning memorable, the idea must be embedded in a story or scenario,"[5] you know that something is happening.

Probably this is just a wave of fashion that will go the way of zero-based budgeting and all the others, but there is a large kernel of truth here nonetheless. Raw data must become information to be used in the formation of knowledge, and knowledge needs to function within a broad base of experience—of the kind that was once called wisdom, in order to be really meaningful. In other words, a woodcutter need only know trees, but to run a park service or a lumber company, you must understand forests as well as trees—to say nothing of markets, public attitudes, and other such elements. Stories can supply such a connecting element.

The value of stories is their versatility, that they can vary in meaning according to circumstances. They are like old-fashioned recipes calling for a "handful" of this and a "walnut-sized" chunk of that rather than giving identically repeatable algorithms. It does not matter that it is simply a matter of the teller and listener projecting their thoughts on to the story rather than the story itself changing.

Here is an example, a story from ancient Benin:

> *Long ago, the Sky was close. So close that people could just reach up and break off a piece. There was good reason to do so, for it could be eaten. People could just reach up, break off a piece, and eat it. Not only could it be eaten, but it had many flavors. One time it would be sweet, another salty, the next time fruity. Unfortunately, people were sometimes careless and would take too much.*
>
> *The Sky God became angry and spoke to the Oba as he sat on his ceremonial stool. Sky God warned the Oba that unless he and his people were more respectful to the sky he would pull away from the earth and leave. All the people were careful after that, for a long time.*

But then, there was a celebration, and, as people walked back to their home villages from the Oba's compound, one person wanted a final taste to make the celebration go on just a little longer, and broke off one last piece. It was too big for one person to eat, so the whole family was called to share it. They were all too full for more than a bite, so all the neighbors were called in also. They were all too tired and sleepy from the dancing and the long walk home, so they could only manage a taste.

Finally, they gave up and threw the last bit away. "Sky won't mind one small piece being wasted, after all it was a celebration and feast—and, anyway, he won't see it." But Sky did and went up to where the sky is now. That was when mankind had to learn how to hunt animals and search for plants to eat.

This story is known as "Why the Sky Is Far Away" and is told in West Africa by descendents of the people of Benin. It is also told in America by African American descendents of those who were carried off into lives of work in slavery, where it is called "Why Men Work." The change in title is revealing.

When I first met the story, I loved it, for it was so human in its laziness and greed—not pathological villainy, but normal, careless, human weakness—taking a little too much, not honoring the source, neglecting to clean up right away. More recently, when I tell it, though, the story is glaringly about the environment and our fears that the earth might stop "her" generosity. Not one word of the story has changed, but the perceptions of those sharing it have.[6]

That flexibility is story's great strength, as well as its vulnerability. Like an optical fiber, a story can carry many internal conversations simultaneously in one fine thread.

Another point to consider is the way a message is presented, and how that affects its acceptability to the hearer. Here is an old Yiddish folktale[7] that addresses this issue.

It seems that Truth was honored by everyone's tongue, but whenever she went to visit people she ended up being given a cold shoulder and found herself back on the street. Parable found her, badly dressed and hungry, and offered to help. Soon Truth was clothed in the costume of story, and the situation changed completely. Now everyone's door was opened to her, and she was welcomed with open arms at parties and quiet evenings alike.

This story always reminds me of another story, about Nasruddin Hodja, the wise fool from Turkey:

Hodja was invited to a fancy dinner party to honor his latest trip to Mecca. On the day of the party he was comforting a grieving villager and ran late, so he went in his old robe. The servant at the door sent him to the kitchen with the other beggars.

He went back home and put on his fancy new robe, then returned to the dinner. This time, he was recognized at the door, and ushered to the head table and served immediately. He said nothing but took a handful from each dish and smeared it on the front of his fancy garments.

Everybody was surprised and asked what he was doing. "Well," said Hodja, "Since it seems to have been my coat that was really being honored, then, it might as well be the one to eat."

So, naked truth is not welcome, but when cloaked in story she finds open doors. The Hodja is invited for his wisdom but shown little respect until arrayed in fine garments. Such stories are a gentle way to get a message across; they allow the hearer to take the idea in with a sense of pleasure rather than with resentment or defensiveness.

The most basic reason of all for storytelling, though, is reflected in a management book:

> Why storytelling?
> Nothing else worked.
> Charts left listeners bemused.
> Prose remained unread.
> Dialogue was just too laborious and slow.
> Time after time, when faced with the task of persuading a group of managers or front-line staff in a large organization to get enthusiastic about a major change, I found that storytelling was the only thing that worked. [8]

Stories are one of the most effective forms of communication humans have ever devised. Using experiential accounts in a knowledge management environment may be new, of course, but those of us who have studied religion and folklore and literature have known story's power for a long time and must be forgiven a little irritation at business types who claim to have re-invented the wheel. Still, the fact of story's efficacy remains, regardless of the setting.

So, stories are a means of addressing complex, ambiguous issues, presenting ideas palatably, and getting the attention of reluctant listeners. They do this by creating a virtual reality that allows the participants to consider something in a laboratory, or what Einstein used to call a "thought experiment."

Beyond their usefulness as teaching tools or pleasant pastimes, stories can be much deeper. They are to a very large extent who we are. Robert Coles, the psychiatrist and writer, in his *The Call of Stories*, quotes Dostoevsky:

> My dear children . . . you must know that there is nothing higher and stronger and more wholesome and good for life in the future than some good memory, especially a memory of childhood, of home. People talk to you a great deal about your education, but some good, sacred memory, preserved from childhood, is perhaps the best education. If one carries many such memories into life, one is safe to the end of one's days,

and if one has only one good memory left in one's heart, even that may be the means of saving us.[9]

Cole goes on to say:

Perhaps Dostoevsky is suggesting that an especially vivid memory itself survives as a monument of factuality (whether or not the memory of a real event)—and helps *us* survive. Without such compelling memories, we are not ourselves, but rather anyone. A memory is an event endowed with the subjectivity of our imaginative life.[10]

Here is another aspect of the virtual reality, of the title. Story can resonate in the memory with such depth that it becomes virtually real, whether "factual" or not, and becomes part of a person's "truth."

The danger is that, for the most part, we are not conscious of the stories we live by. There are stories about New York that keep some people "safely" on Long Island and give those of us that live in the city a false sense of glamour about our lives' bravery and excitement.[11] There are stories that have some people seeking a doctorate in pursuit of "the good life" in terms of a good job with status and money and others pursuing "a good life" in terms of "meaningful existence and wisdom." Guess what? All these stories can both be true and false and all can co-exist.

The Nigerian-born novelist Ben Okri has said:

It is easy to forget how mysterious and mighty stories are. They do their work in silence, invisibly. They work with all the internal materials of the mind and self. They become part of you while changing you. Beware the stories you read or tell: subtly, at night, beneath the waters of consciousness, they are altering your world. [12]

The tales we tell ourselves have powerful impact, and this is as true of us as groups as it is of us as individuals. I often wonder how our age will look to the future. The entertainment industry is currently indulging our taste for raps of rage that have replaced the sentimental croonings of earlier generations and is feeding our insatiable hunger for virtual violence in entertainment. As a child, I can remember feeling shocked by the Roman culture with its gladiators, but now it is quite normal again—just shown "virtually" in film or acted out by the World Wrestling Entertainment. We can watch cruel deaths any night of the week, with popcorn, and without leaving the comfort of our own sofa.

Rollo May and other modern psychologists have talked in great depth about the role of myth in all our lives, and I strongly recommend his *The Cry for Myth*[13] to anyone interested in the importance of myth. But what I want to consider now is how we construct our view of ourselves through "true" stories, "true" in the sense of factual rather than that of carrying moral truths. There is one phrase from that quote from Robert Coles that haunts me: "Without such compelling memories, we are not ourselves, but rather anyone."

Feinstein and Kippner say:

> The diversity of the mythic images we encounter through electronic and other media can also be overwhelming. For most of the history of civilization, the myths held by the individuals in a society were relatively uniform. . . . However, no single unifying force in today's complex civilization is powerful enough to preserve cohesion amid the multitude of competing myths and fragments of myths people are exposed to now.
>
> It is likely that your attitudes and values differ from your neighbors' in ways that could not even have been conceived in tribal cultures. In addition, you have been obliged to learn how to reflect on the fit between your myths and the situations you encounter with more agility than your parents or the generations before them. Never have so many visions been available to choose from, nor has there been media so capable of parading those visions in front of you. Growing up is no longer a matter of following in the well-tried footsteps of ancestors who may for generations have been in the same trade, held similar religious convictions, and considered the tradition-

bound roles of men and women to be part of the natural order.[14]

Sam Keen put it this way:

> We are the first generation bombarded with so many stories from so many "authorities," none of which are our own. The parable of the postmodern mind is the person surrounded by a media center: three television screens in front of them giving three sets of stories; fax machines bringing in other stories; newspapers providing still more stories. In a sense, we are saturated with stories; we're saturated with points of view. But the effect of being bombarded with all of these points of view is that we don't have a point of view and we don't have a story. We lose the continuity of our experiences; we become people who are written on from the outside.[15]

It is not just individuals but entire cultures that define themselves in symbols and stories. As a species we seem to keep defining ourselves in terms of the culture's current obsession—a broader version of the old dictum: "To the man with a hammer, all looks like a nail." If you think in terms of mechanics, you see the human organism as a kind of machine; if you think of computers, you see the human brain as something that computes. (Notice that even those most concerned with the rational are here thinking in metaphors.)

So, what is it we think, now? Now we are in an era of artificial intelligence and virtual reality.

One expert in artificial intelligence, Roger Schank, says something very similar to what Cole said:

> We tell stories to describe ourselves not only so others can understand who we are but also so we can understand ourselves. "Telling our stories allows us to compile our personal mythology, and the collection of stories we have compiled is to some extent who we are, what we have to say about the world, and tells the world the state of our mental health."

To some extent, our stories, because they are shaped by
memory processes that do not always have their basis in
hard fact, are all fictions. But these fictions are based on
real experiences and are our only avenue to these experiences. [16]

So, according to Schank, "the collection of stories we have com-
piled is to some extent who we are . . . " He also talks about how
we can define ourselves through others' stories. As an example,
he discusses one televangelist and the stories he tells that have so
many aspects that hearers can connect to and identify with.
Schank is very critical of this kind of story, meant to sell, but the
issue is important. He says:

When we hear the stories of others, the issue becomes whether
we choose to adopt these stories for ourselves. We define ourselves through our own stories, but through teaching (and
preaching), we also define ourselves through the stories of
others. Many people who are good storytellers know how to
take advantage of this basic human need to define oneself
through the stories other people live.

The stories of our culture are those stories that we hear so often that they cease to seem like stories to us. They are the stories that we take for granted. They are the stories we live by.
The more independent we are, the more the stories we tell that
are uniquely our own. The more connected with others that we
wish to be, the more the stories we tell are those that are already well understood by our listeners . . . [17]

Schank has written much about computers and learning; this
comes from: *Tell Me a Story: A New Look at Real and Artificial
Memory*. He follows that thought with:

The issue for anyone interested in intelligence, then, is
what behaviors signify intelligence.
For years I have been fascinated by the seemingly intrin-
sic human desire to tell a good story. . . . We assess the intelli-

gence of others on the basis of the stories that they tell and on the basis of their receptivity to our own stories. . . . Finding the right ones (memories of experiences), having the right ones come to mind at the right times, having created accounts of the right ones in anticipation of their eventual use in this way, are all significant aspects of intelligent behavior . . .[18]

People think in terms of stories. They understand the world in terms of stories that they have already understood. New events or problems are understood by reference to old previously understood stories and explained to others by the use of stories. . . . Scientists have prototypical scientific success and failure stories that they use to help them with new problems. Historians have their favorite stories in terms of which they understand and explain the world . . . [19]

If all you recall is the rule, it will be hard to figure out what to do when the rule fails. But if the story that generated the rule is still available, you can look at the data again and create a new rule . . .

Intelligence, for machines as well as for humans, is the telling of the right story at the right time in the right way.[20]

These are heady words for those of us who have loved story and have had to swallow a lot of scorn from technotypes who dismiss stories as a waste of time. But then that cockiness has been a large part of the technology story since the first computer nerd suddenly realized that he had power. I was very amused to see in *Forbes ASAP* an article by Michael Wolff called "Got It?"[21] He tells his story:

Early on, I was attracted to the technology business because I really thought it represented an inner circle of understanding.

"Getting it" was an accurate way to describe this inner circle of understanding, because it was like getting a joke. It was a riff; That is there was no real knowledge that you had to possess . . . it was closer to a religious truth or a cultural truth. It was an insider's thing . . .

At the first technology conference I ever went to, in late 1991, I heard statements that were mesmerizing in their absolutism, in their verbal forcefulness, in their aphoristic neatness: "Everything is changing, and change is good." ". . . speed changes the meaning of information." "Technology makes the weak strong."

It was an authority thing. The question was: Do you get the fact that power was passing to different people, that new cats were taking over? . . . it was a little like how it must have felt in the '30s to be an agitated student first hearing Marxist philosophy. Here was a new point of view that seemed to explain everything. It was the big picture. Comprehensive. Global. Here was a coherent theory of modern life. What's more, it didn't leave room for anyone else's point of view . . . You were either the future or the ash heap.

There weren't a lot of people who could stand up to this intellectual aggressiveness and verbal abuse. I wish I could communicate, however guilty I feel about it now, the sheer joy of sitting in meetings with well-established businessmen representing billions of dollars of assets. . . . And being able not only to high hand them . . . but . . . flagrantly condescend to them like children . . .[22]

Getting it, I believe, is a conceit on the part of people who are overly enamored with what technology can do. It is a form of snobbery. . . . But at the same time, we should not underestimate the extent to which the myth of getting it is just an ordinary hustle . . .

It isn't, necessarily, that what was being said and sold by the people who claimed to get it was untrue. But it was true in the sense that astrology is often true. Things would change. Sure. Duh. And then ? . . . [23]

Wow. What a story! It is not often that one reads such an "in your face" look in the mirror as Wolff's. Here, clearly, is a story that is being told in our lifetime. So, the technotypes are now questioning their story about "getting it" and business types are now "getting it" about story.

But back to virtual reality again. If one thinks about it, all literature is virtual reality. It is, however, of the imagination, not computer based, so we discount it in our technology-drunk time. Guess what? Shakespeare "got it." Listen to the prologue of Henry V:

O for a Muse of fire, that would ascend
The brightest heaven of invention,
A kingdom for a stage, princes to act
And monarchs to behold the swelling scene!
. . . But pardon, and gentles all,
The flat unraised spirits that have dared
On this unworthy scaffold to bring forth
So great an object: can this cockpit hold
The vasty fields of France? or may we cram
Within this wooden O the very casques
That did affright the air at Agincourt?
O, pardon! since a crooked figure may
Attest in little place a million;
And let us, ciphers to this great accompt,
On your imaginary forces work . . .

Piece out our imperfections with your thoughts;
Into a thousand parts divide one man,
And make imaginary puissance;
Think when we talk of horses, that you see them
Printing their proud hoofs i' the receiving earth;
For 'tis your thoughts that now must deck our kings,
Carry them here and there; jumping o'er times,
Turning the accomplishment of many years
Into an hour-glass . . .[24]

I wonder whether Shakespeare would see, in film and virtual reality machines, his "muse of fire?" Nor is it just high culture and that uses virtual reality. Someone in a recent conversation introduced the issue of child pornography created in virtual reality, in which no real children are affected. The question becomes, of course, whether we find pedophilia objectionable because children are harmed or because it is morally or aesthetically offensive even in the abstract. What brought me up short was someone saying: "But all pornography is virtual reality. It allows people to fantasize without having to deal with the 'stuff' that comes with reality."[25]

That was a startling thought. It brought to mind a book concerned with how we are becoming more and more isolated and less trusting as we converse less face-to-face with friends and acquaintances and interface more and more with strangers through technology. John Locke's *Why We Don't Talk to Each Other Anymore: The De-Voicing of Society* [26] says:

> The social feedback mechanisms that were handed down by our evolutionary ancestors—systems that were designed and carefully tuned by hundreds of millennia of face-to-face interaction—are rarely used nowadays, and there is a potential for miscommunication and mistrust as never before in human history. [27]
>
> If you are autistic, welcome to the voiceless society. It was tailor-made for you. If you enjoy typing "I L-O-V-E Y-O-U" to a faceless stranger, a blissful future lies ahead. But if, like the rest of us, you need to share yourself with others, to enjoy the intimate company of close friends, and to be deeply understood, you may have already begun to miss the sound of social calls. You may be devoicing. [28]

Locke may use some exaggeration for effect, but there is also much truth in what he says. Perhaps what we really need is a new version of *Don Quixote*. Cervantes was mocking the dangers of people getting seduced into madness with books full of adventure and heroism. Many scholars say that it was this very book that gave birth to the novel. It's hard, now, to remember that once upon a time, children were scolded for reading too much, and warned that "reading rots the brain." That sprang from the fear that reading was too solitary an activity. Now there is a new level to that isolation. What *would* a cyber-Don Q. look like, I wonder?

So, from the shared virtual reality of storytelling utilizing the shared imagination of teller and told, to the book with its sharing separated in time and space, to the fragmentation of technological telling, to . . . now, in the corporate and academic worlds, a call back to traditional storytelling. Human nature really hasn't changed.

Story has provided a means for imagining possible answers since our beginnings. The apparent capriciousness of the gods can be revealed, if not fully explained, important essentials can be made memorable, and potential situations and their possible outcomes can be explored. Commercial film companies may have laid claim to the Dream Factory, but in fact each person has his or her own wish-fulfillment factory and the means of satisfying justice internally.

Story can answer many needs and questions, whether it is the metaphor or symbol that provides the essence of the solution to a scientist's problem or the full-blown story that satisfies an unmet emotional hunger. One may dream of revenge or justice, of personal glory, or peace. The choice of what to turn into story is an individual matter, but it is there for each of us. No batteries are needed, only a willingness to listen, an imagination, and an open heart. It happens whether we are conscious of it or not, whether we are cynical or naïve. If we are our stories, then story must be recognized as the powerful tool it is and used wisely. Let us remember that the study of information covers not only documents of data but also the glimpses of truth and wisdom recorded as story.

Notes

1. Stephen Crane, "The Wayfarer" (1899) *War Is Kind & Other Lines* (Mineola, N.Y.: Dover, 1998).

2. Emery Roe, *Narrative Policy Analysis: Theory and Practice* (Durham, N.C.: Duke University Press, 1994).

3. B. Joseph Pine II and James H. Gilmore, *The Experience Economy: Work Is Theatre & Every Business a Stage* (Boston, Mass.: Harvard Business School Press, 1999).

4. Stephen Denning, *The Springboard: How Storytelling Ignites Action in Knowledge-Era Organizations* (Oxford: Butterworth / Heinemann, 2001).

5. John Seely Brown, A. Collins, and Paul Duguid, "Situated Cognition and the Culture of Learning." *Educational Technology*, 18 no. 1 (January.February,1989).

6. The first version I read had a woman be the one who broke the bond, but other versions have it as a man or a child. Rather than evoke the Western connotation of the Biblical story of Eve who lost us Paradise, I usually just identify the character as a "person." It was included as: "Why the Sky Is Far Away," in *The Origin of Life and Death: African Creation Myths*, edited by Ulli Beier (London: Heinemann, 1966). Mary Joan Gerson did a picture book version, that came out in two editions, illustrated by different artists: Mary-Joan Gerson, *Why the Sky Is Far Away: A Folktale from Nigera*, illustrated by Hope Meryman (New York: Harcourt, 1974), and Mary-Joan Gerson, *Why the Sky Is Far Away: A Nigerian Folktale*, illustrated by Carla Golembe (Boston: Little Brown, 1992). The African American version can be found in several places, including: Julius Lester, *Black Folk Tales*, illustrated by Tom Feelings (New York: Baron, 1969).

7. It is attributed to Rabbi Jacob Kranz, an 18th century Eastern European storyteller and teacher who was also known as the Maggid of Dubbno. It can be found in Ausubel's *A Treasury of Jewish Folktales* (New York: Galahad, 1993).

8. Denning, *The Springboard*, xiii.

9. Fyodor Doestoevsky, Speaking as Alyosha in *The Brother's Karamazov*. Quoted in Robert Coles, *The Call of Stories: Teaching and the Moral Imagination* (Boston: Houghton Mifflin, 1989), 183.

10. Robert Coles, *The Call of Stories: Teaching and the Moral Imagination* (Boston: Houghton Mifflin, 1989), 183.

11. This was presented just a few months before September 11, 2001. Now, of course there are different New York stories, of real courage and tragedy.

12. Ben Okri, no. 58, "Aphorisms and Fragments: The Joy of Story-telling," *Birds of Heaven* (NewYork: Phoenix, 1996).

13. Rollo May, *The Cry for Myth* (New York: Delta, 1992 [1991]).

14. David Feinstein and Stanley Krippner, *Personal Mythology: The Psychology of Your Evolving Self* (Los Angeles, Calif.: Targer/Perigee, 1988), 7.

15. Sam Keen. Quoted at: www.tech-head.com/story.htm (5 January 2001).

16. Roger C. Schank, *Tell Me a Story: A New Look at Real and Artificial Memory* (New York: Scribners, 1990), 44.

17. Schank, *Tell Me a Story*, 218.

18. Schank, Preface, *Tell Me a Story*, xi.

19. Schank, *Tell Me a Story*, 219

20. Schank, *Tell Me a Story*, 241-2.

21. Michael Wolff, "Got It?" *Forbes ASAP* issue 5 (2 October 2000) Issue devoted to "What is True?," 37-38.

22. Wolff, "Got It?," 37.

23. Wolff, "Got It?," 38.

24. Shakespeare. Prologue. *Henry V.* Renascence editions. www.uoregon.edu/~rbear/shake/hv.html (7 January 2002).

25. Tom Wiser. He has a bachelors in folklore from Harvard and a masters in computer science. In conversation, (14 February, 2001).

26. John Locke, *Why We Don't Talk to Each Other Anymore: The De-Voicing of Society* (New York: Touchstone, 1998). The cover adds: "How e-mail, voice mail, the internet, and technomania are making us into a society of strangers." It seems to also have been distributed as: *The De-Voicing of Society, Why We Don't Talk to Each Other Anymore.*

27. Locke, *Why We Don't Talk to Each Other Anymore*, 19.

28. Locke, *Why We Don't Talk to Each Other Anymore*, 20.

Chapter 8

Ironworker or Ancient Mariner: Tales that Must Be Told

Introduction to the Talk

This was originally delivered at the School of Library and Information Science, Catholic University of America. Washington, D.C., February 8, 2002

The dean of the School of Library and Information Science at the Catholic University of America invited me to teach a storytelling class in spring of 2002. I thought he wanted me to teach the Myth in the Information Age class, and, being consumed with the current events of September 11, 2001, I thought about the relevance of current events to story. When it turned out that what was scheduled was a how-to course, I offered to turn my philosophical thoughts into a lecture for the class and any one else from the school who was interested. "Ironworker" is the result. This is the only talk addressed primarily to people interested in becoming tellers, and the only one to seriously discuss personal stories.

Clearly I was still recovering from having been an eyewitness to September 11, 2001, and its aftermath, and needed to tell

*my own story about a story. The students, when asked to intro-
duce themselves in story told deeply moving personal stories of
tragedies and struggles for truth, rather than the usual amusing
anecdotes that begin most storytelling classes. That tone of in-
tensity remains in this chapter; it is to be hoped that readers will
be tolerant.*

*The story of the Seven Sleepers of Ephesus is one that I
learned for a story concert I did as a Benjamin Dean Lecture for
the Planetarium of the California Academy of Science in San
Francisco. It has haunted me since I met it, perhaps because I
had loved visiting the ruins at Ephesus.*

Ironworker or Ancient Mariner:
Tales that Must Be Told

I AM AN
IRONWORKER
I helld [sic] *you in my hands*
I did not know who you were
+ now I am showererd [sic] *clean*
but yet I still feel dirty
I don't know why,
but I feel ashamed
Who were you?[1]

Clearly, I am neither an ironworker nor part of the cleanup crew, but I am a New Yorker and was an eyewitness to the crash of the Twin Towers of the World Trade Center. I found myself completely helpless, unable even to offer comfort to the grieving strangers I stood with, in midtown, as we smelled the smoke and watched the fire. What could anyone say to the Russian woman whose mother worked on an upper floor of Tower One? Or to the man who silently dropped his cell phone and shook his head as he lost contact with the friend who was on his way down the stairs of Tower Two as we watched it crumble?

I understand the shame felt by this ironworker who wrote this poem, for I felt it too. It is called survivor guilt. All the sympathy I have felt, then and since, is genuine, but still I am glad I was not in the building and that those I am closest to made it out safely.

What does this have to do with storytelling? Everything, and nothing. The ironworker's statement, written anonymously on the sidewalk, reveals one of the bare roots shared by poetry and story: the experiencing of something so deep that it must be shared. Somehow, a witness is needed. The "Ancient Mariner who stoppeth one of three,"[2] really *must* tell his tale.

If I had any doubts about the therapeutic role story can have for the teller, it stopped the day I saw this scribbled on the cobblestones at Union Square. Part of such an experience is simply trying to come to grips with reality, and talking can support the part of you that knows what happened but can't yet believe it. It can help the rest of you begin to let it *feel* real. Expressing it in words helps you to externalize it and be able to grasp it intellectually. Part of it is having yourself validated, whatever role you had in an occasion; simply being seen and mirrored is proof that you still exist, even in a state of shock.

Emily Dickinson caught this need to see a situation in the third person:

> A doubt if it be Us
> Assists the staggering Mind
> In an extremer Anguish
> Until it footing find.
>
> An Unreality is lent,
> A merciful Mirage
> That makes the living possible
> While it suspends the lives.[3]

A different part of the desire to share such an experience is the need to explain to others what happened, to let them know how important it was. This need to share information as narrative seems to be crucial to human beings. One scientist who works in artificial intelligence even thinks that telling stories could be what defines us as human beings.[4] Whether that is so or not, telling stories is an essentially human activity.

How much of telling and explaining is hoping the hearer will have an answer, or can offer absolution for your role, and how much is just the need for sharing the feeling, I do not know, but shutting down and not talking seems to put people at greater risk of not recovering from trauma. This need to share one's story with a sympathetic listener is one of the factors that make self-help groups like the twelve-step programs, in which people exchange their stories, so powerful.

Not all stories can have happy endings, and it is important to tell history as well as well as imaginative tales. This is an aspect of storytelling less common today in our news broadcasting world: the attempt to capture an event in words for those who were not there. That was the role of the bards, who, like Homer or Shakespeare, recounted battles and wars, so that, as Henry V says:

And gentlemen in England now-a-bed
Shall think themselves accurs'd they were not here,
And hold their manhoods cheap whiles any speaks
That fought with us upon Saint Crispin's day.[5]

It is hard for us, so accustomed to print and media, to remember that we were humans for millennia before written history began. Oral tradition honored great stories, those that really mattered, by passing them down, from generation to generation. Like a kind of intellectual genetic code, the DNA of stories that worked survived and spread, while the less "fit" lasted only within a small group or for a limited time. Notice the use of the word "fit" rather than "best," since, as a consequence of the very phenomenon we are discussing, we have no way of knowing what great tales and ideas were lost during this evolution of oral tradition to literature.

The means of capturing and telling stories has also changed. The reason I can quote the "I am an ironworker" statement here is because I bought a photograph of it from Here is New York,[6] the photo gallery that appeared on Spring Street shortly after September 11, 2001 to show pictures related to the World Trade Center and the events surrounding it. There were thousands of photos there—on the wall, piled on tables, hanging from strings like wash on a line—all being looked at, reverently, by people who had lined up, patiently, around the block, to await their turn. I had only enough cash to buy one picture and had seen many that moved me deeply, but when I saw this there was no question. "Trust you to go to a photo exhibit and buy a picture of words," I shook my head at myself. Nevertheless, I was deeply grateful that someone had caught those evanescent words, long since washed off by the rain.

Since then I have spoken with that photographer, who drove twenty-four hours straight to get back home to New York and offer help. He, too, found the words scribbled on the cobblestones at Union Square deeply moving, and as a storyteller of image wanted to preserve them.

Technologies such as the camera offer great new means of sharing story, but their product and impact are quite different. It really is difficult for us to understand how abnormal our technology makes us from the perspective of most of humankind throughout history (and pre-history). I heartily recommend Walter Ong's *Orality and Literacy: The Technologizing of the Word* [7] for a full discussion of the impact of print on the ways we think, both as individuals and as cultures. Marshall McLuhan and others have talked about how media in some ways mimics oral cultures, but it is not really the same.

Simply, we cannot unknow the fact that material is available in text form. We assume that we can have access to whatever we want, including the prediction of tomorrow's weather. We take it for granted and are irritated by its absence rather than awed by its availability.

Try to translate information into money, for an analogy. A millionaire would find it very hard to truly imagine the poverty a slum dweller knows all too well. But wealth and poverty, both, would be hard to understand for someone who lives within a barter system without money.

The post-modern world can be seen as a global village or as one with enclaves of modernity and privilege if you prefer to think in terms of *Information Inequality* [8] but not everyone in the world accepts either perspective, because some don't see information as central to life. This conviction that "information" holds all the answers to life seems self-evident at the moment, but this attitude is really a fairly recent phenomenon. My grandmother, for instance, was sent to college at the turn of the last century in Washington State, not because she was the brightest in the family, but because she was sickly and therefore would never be chosen as a wife by any man of sense. Giving her an education so that she could earn a living as a teacher was the best the family could do for her. As it happens, they were wrong and she did marry, but the point remains. Everything changes; what seems unquestionable today may seem quaint tomorrow, as situations and attitudes change.

Since we are all still trying to absorb what happened a few months ago and ponder the whys, let's think about the differences between the technologically based world view we have in the United States and that of the religion-based perspective of the Taliban and Al-Quada. It would seem that they see their lives in continuity with Muhammed and jihad. They may use modern technological tools, but the mindset is traditional, and education is still as much oral recitation more than written.

In contrast, the Crusades feel very far away to us, in time as well as place (at least I hope that's still so). Our view of history as a straight line "from then to now . . . and on into the future" does not work in an oral culture for which time revolves in a continuous circle of seasons rather than going forward. Our stories tend to be about the future, which is unusual to most of human story that tends to look to the past or outside time in "once upon a time."

I will come back to the Middle East later, but want to follow this discussion of time further and mention Guy Debord, who believes that our being in a corporate-run media-based world has changed us so that we have reverted from the modern sense of time. His idea is that we have lost all our sense of history and are stuck in a constant "now," with current fashion and constant innovation being what matters. As the song had it: "Who wants yesterday's paper?"[9] We feel there is no time to consider what has happened and what it might mean in light of similar situations from the past; there is barely enough time to focus on what we are concerned with—the immediate future. According to him and his Situationists, we have lost our historical perspective and most rational judgment with it.

The perception of time is just one side effect of what Debord calls our shift to the "spectacular" society. Writing in the 1960s, he combined the kind of leftist French pessimism of the existentialists with the awareness of the impact of media on the modern world that we in North America associate with Marshall McLuhan. In his *The Society of the Spectacle,*[10] Debord begins:

> In societies where modern conditions of production prevail, all of life presents itself as an immense accumulation of *spectacles.* Everything that was directly lived has moved away into a representation.

More and more of our life is spent buying services or watching others do, professionally, what we used to do for ourselves. Just a few examples are necessary to demonstrate his point: sports, which we used to play rather than watch as professional matches; music, which used to take the form of singing around a piano as a group, rather than watching MTV; or games, which used to be played between people rather than watched as game shows or played against computers. What about eating? Food that used to be prepared at home is now eaten in restaurants, delivered, or bought pre-prepared and frozen. Cooking from scratch is now kept for special occasions.

In 1988 Debord wrote *Comments on The Society of the Spectacle,*[11] looking at the way his hypotheses of twenty years before had been playing out. Certainly, it seems that the trends he noticed are increasing. One of the consequences he noted in particular is that we now look externally for meaning and allow news broadcasts and editorials to take the place of discussions of issues and policies. In other words, we are letting others think and develop opinions for us, simply choosing to listen to those groups that most closely fit our personal tastes.

The Situationists, reflecting their political views, see this opinion shaping as being consciously manipulated by corporate interests who find it easier to work with passive participants in this "spectacular society." I am not convinced that any "they" is in control, although some may like to see themselves that way, and I am not so sure that most people of earlier generations were really so much more likely to ponder issues.

At any rate, however, it is clear that who we are as humans has certainly changed. People like Donna Haraway[12] believe that we have gone way beyond this anyway, that we are no longer simply humans, but have become part cyborg with all our technological extensions of self. Certainly, many individuals seem incomplete without walkmans or cell phones glued to their ears and mouths to add technology-mediated input by ear and output by mouth. Most of the overheard conversations sound pretty inane; it is almost as if some of these people need constant feedback regardless of the content. This takes us back to where we began. Whether or not society is technologized, we still seem to need to tell each other about our lives.

The emphasis, earlier, on the beneficial role of storytelling for the teller could be misinterpreted as slighting those who tell personal stories. Far from it, the courage of those who publicly tell personal stories, particularly painful ones, is enormous, involving great risk and vulnerability, in reaching out to others who might be addressing related "stories" in their own lives or those of people about whom they care. And these stories can do great good for their listeners. It is simply to point out that telling can be of benefit to the teller and that it seems to be an inherent part of being human. If we were all good at telling our stories, life might well be easier and would certainly be more entertaining. If we practiced more and learned its skills, maybe more of us could be good tellers.

Nor is it just that we have a need to tell. There has been an enormous growth in the appetite for hearing personal stories on the part of audiences. This phenomenon fascinates me. Where does it come from and why are traditional stories being replaced by these personal stories? I believe that it springs in large part from the same thing that Debord was talking about, that we are in many ways being isolated by technology and consequently feel real hunger for human discourse. More and more of us are silently watching talk shows where others are interacting. Fewer and fewer of us are experiencing dinner table conversation with people telling family stories or discussing issues.

Debord discusses at length the important connection between reading and thinking, but the connection between listening and understanding is even more basic. It is really no surprise that those of us lucky enough to remember sitting on a front porch talking, or better yet, listening to an oldster telling stories are attracted to places like the National Storytelling Festival. There we can listen to the best of raconteurs telling polished versions of funny, touching or heartwarming stories about people.

Earlier we were discussing the stories that must be told. Now we are talking about those that are told for entertainment and the enjoyment of the shared experience, whether as teller or audience. It is almost like being invited to a family picnic and hearing about all the funny things those crazy relatives did, knowing that the laughter is a shared laughter of affection, not the cynical mocking of scorn. Few can resist the appeal of such tales.

Preparing such stories, amusing or tender, is very hard work, however, for rarely does life present incidents with clearly demarcated beginnings, middles and ends, or complete with proper pacing and amusing fillers or transitions. The talent for story constructing is not always connected to that of storytelling, which is probably part of why so many authors hate speaking and so many storytellers stick to folktales.

Beyond questions of talent, and the difficulty of overcoming a reticence to talk about one's own life, lie the many issues that come up with this kind of personal tale. There is the issue of how much "embroidery" is appropriate. Having heard great tellers tell very different stories incorporating the same incidents, it is clear that story crafting plays a big part. With stories told for sheer entertainment that does not matter, but when they are "healing stories," that are addressed to an audience waiting to hear that problems are survivable and believing that these stories are "true," it matters a great deal. Integrity really matters when listeners open their hearts to a teller, as happens with healing stories, whether factual or traditional. Ellis, one of our premier storytellers and workshop teachers, often talks of the responsibility of the teller to "bring the listeners safely home" when they have trusted that teller on a journey into story.

A similar issue is that of telling stories that are not one's own. Ellis[13] tells people in her workshops of such an incident involving her son, Scooter. She has, for years, told a story[14] that deals with a thorny point in his life (and her own) and has even recorded it on audiotape. Scooter was passing through a shopping mall one day and overheard another teller relating that same story. He was, not surprisingly, angry and challenged the teller, saying, in effect: "that is not your story, that is my mother's story, and I know that because the boy in the story is me and you do not have my permission to tell it." Some people seem to be unable to distinguish between personal life stories shaped for public telling and public domain folklore.

Disregarding the copyright issues, we are left with simple ethical issues. What has happened that we don't think of stories as belonging to someone? Is it because we are so used to recounting movie plots that are copyright material but that we are encouraged to retell for the sake of "word-of-mouth" publicity? Is it because we are so used to things being presented technologically (as part of Debord's spectacular society) that the idea that a real person is telling a story that really happened and that still has emotional content for the teller and participants just doesn't occur to us? Is it that we are too narcissistic to care? Or is it that we have come to a time when we must be creative secondhand, like tracing pictures or painting by number—or by rotely memorizing something heard on a tape? Granted, oral tradition is based on generation after generation of hearers repeating the stories they have heard, but there are stories and stories. Many cultures respect story as a form of property, belonging to the teller. If that teller dies without passing on the right to tell the story, then that story dies, too, and its ghost disappears once those who remember it are gone. That is hard for us to understand, but it is true in many cultures.

An alternative type of personal story is the kind that is personal for the listener, custom made, as it were. Those bedtime stories, told by parents, often with the child listener featured as protagonist, or with a set of characters that appear in an ongoing saga, are a prime example. Some of these stories have gone on into book form, for example Beatrix Potter's Peter Rabbit, and A.A. Milne's Winnie-the-Pooh. These are in print, now, but they maintain their origins by being shared as bedtime read-alouds so they are heard rather than read silently.

James Thurber's character Walter Mitty and his elaborate daydreams involving himself as a variety of heroes presents another guise of personal story. Which of us has not retold, at one time or another, to our own ears or another's what should have happened, or what we should have said to some obnoxious person? This may be neurotic, but it is a very satisfying activity, and may well be another root of storytelling.

Related, but quite different, is the fascinating form of storytelling begun by Milton Erickson with his Ericksonian Hypnosis. This therapy demands that the therapist be an expert storyteller, for it requires a story that fits the situation to a "T." After getting to know the patient and his issues, the therapist hypnotizes the patient and tells him a story, not featuring the patient directly, but a character with whom the patient's subconscious can easily identify. The story then takes that character into a situation that is analogous to the issue being addressed. For example, someone dealing with the sense of being trapped in a job or a marriage might hear of a character being stuck in a tight place, like a tunnel or a subway turnstile. As the story progresses, a variety of possible outcomes are introduced, but never completed, so that the patient's own unconscious can choose what resolution seems most satisfying. Of course, this is a gross over-simplification of the process, and extra help is offered along the way, but it is a very interesting form of therapy developed by a psychiatrist who seems to have had amazing success with many patients, and it does suggest that stories are really integral to healthy human life.

For cultures as a whole, the fable and religious parable play a similar role. Listening to a story does not seem like being preached at, but the lesson is there to be learned by anyone who chooses to listen and finds it relevant to a situation. For example, there is a fable of a man, his son and their donkey. First he rides and is criticized for riding while the boy with his short legs must walk, then the boy rides and the criticism is of the boy's lack of respect for his father, then they both ride and people complain of the cruelty to the donkey. Finally they carry the donkey, and everyone laughs at their stupidity. The story gets the point across: it is impossible to satisfy everyone all the time. It works as well now as it did in ancient Greece.

Beyond telling one's own stories or having stories told specifically for us, there is a third way stories can become "personal stories." I have a good friend who is a storyteller and used to tell a particular transformation tale all the time—until she resolved a life decision about changing careers and then no longer found that particular story of interest and stopped telling it. That attachment to a particular story can happen several times in a lifetime. According to many psychologists, we need to hear stories as children in order to develop a sense of who we are becoming. The main source of this kind of tale is myth and folktale. These tales contain matter that the human subconscious still seems to need.

Theoretically, we are attracted to stories that address the developmental issues we are currently dealing with. The pull between safety and independence is addressed in Little Red Riding Hood, for example. Or, for another example, sibling rivalry couldn't be much more blatantly represented than in the Old Testament story of Joseph and his jealous brothers, who sold him into slavery over his father's gift of a handsome coat of many colors.

Some of the best stories are hero tales, meant to fill a listener with dreams and hope and courage. Most hero tales are action stories, but heroes can face many different kinds of challenges. In a media age, many of the heroes are real people, and that means getting to hear of their weaknesses as well as their greatness. That changes the impact in some ways, but it still remains significant. Think about it; how many of us have used stories to encourage ourselves in seeking some goal? How many boys have longed to join King Arthur's round table? How many girls have been inspired by the stories of Marie Curie or Florence Nightingale?

Cynicism seems clever at the moment, but I sometimes wonder whether the self-involved Rugrats and over-sophisticated South Park kids are all we have to offer the next generation as role models? I do not say that children should not watch television, or that they should only read "nice" stories about virtue, but they should be offered a variety of appealing positive perspectives as well as sophisticated negative ones.

Maybe a good cautionary myth for our age and the Society of the Spectacle would be the story of King Midas. He so hungered for gold that when offered a wish he chose that everything he should touch would turn to gold. When his wish was granted, he faced starvation and had to watch his beloved lively daughter turn into a statue as she touched him. In a spectacular society, perhaps the girl is more likely to turn into a robot or a clone than a gold statue, but the principle remains the same, that our children are being affected by our age's obsessions.

It is my belief that old-fashioned storytelling is one of the best defenses against the dangers of the Society of the Spectacle. It offers a real person-to-person experience and provides material for internal nourishment that has not been processed or turned to gold but is left as "real ingredients," for minds and hearts to turn into living ideas.

My belief is strong, but with it comes a strong warning. Like all things of power, stories are not always used for good, or by the good. Many business interests have discovered the impact of story and are using it in ways that distress me, similar to the constant wrapping up of products in the flag that we have seen in the past few months.

This brings us to where we began. I want to end this with a particular story to reclaim it for myself. It is a medieval Christian legend, but because takes place in what is now Turkey it has been adopted by Muslim tradition as well. Catholic University seems a good site for reclaiming it.

Long ago, during Decius' day in Rome, Ephesus had a reputation for being a wonderful place, with beautiful views of the sea, beyond rolling hills. It also had a lovely climate, with bright blue skies and just enough rain for lovely flowers and trees with delicious fruit. The city was beautiful itself, because it was built with nearby marble that was lovely and bright in the sun. It also had an interesting culture, formed by its position close to the Greek Islands, but on the Asian coast, so that it was full of people from many backgrounds who had stopped on their way to or from Rome going further east or south to Lebanon or Egypt.

Decius had heard of these wonders, but also had heard disturbing stories of people who refused to worship at his new temple. Now, no one would mind if you want to worship Astarte or Dionysus or any other god, as long as you paid due honor the Emperor, who was after all a living god. These people worshiped a carpenter, and not even from a place anyone had heard of, from Galilee or some such place. They called themselves Christians, after him. But this carpenter was dead! Imagine how crazy they had to be to value a dead carpenter more highly than a living emperor!

Well, Decius decided that the time had come to visit Ephesus, and he came, along with many of his court. When they arrived and set up court there, he found that it was indeed a lovely place, and the food presented by all those cooks from all those countries using the fresh local produce was well worth the trip. Unfortunately, the other stories about the city were also true. Even with the Emperor present, there were still people who did not offer their proper tribute. Decius liked Ephesus and did not want to be unnecessarily harsh, but there are limits. So he invited all to come to the temple to honor him, but made it a celebration. Most came, for what harm would it do; and any reasonable god would understand and not be jealous.

There were a few of those Christians, though, that still held out, and it became necessary to pass laws threatening imprisonment and even death to those who would not comply. Then began a terrible time, with families splitting and turning one against the other, and turning each other in, out of fear. One day, Decius happened to visit the court as seven young men were brought before the judge. They looked clear of eye and of conscience and, from the way they were dressed and the way they spoke, proudly and correctly, it was obvious that they were all from wealthy local families, although their names made it clear that the families were of many background.

Decius suddenly decided that these would make much better ornaments to his court than sacrifices to their beliefs, so, before they had committed themselves to refusing to worship him, he stood and announced that court would be suspended for a week while he went on a boar hunt. He looked at the young men and said they should spend the night in jail, and then spend the week considering their answer. He knew that what can be done with pride in the face of friends, often weakens in the night, alone—especially when there are prisoners being tortured nearby, and the frightened imagination can do its work.

So, the next day, Decius went on his hunt, and the seven young men were released from prison. They were not shaken, but went about their affairs, saying goodbye to family and friends and selling their goods to give to the poor, keeping only enough coins to make a long stay in prison more bearable. On the last day before they were to reappear in court, they met together at a cave where they had used to play together as children. It was iso-

lated and had a good view of the far away sea, so it would be a good place to spend their last night of freedom, and maybe of life, praying and fasting and meditating on their beliefs. The only creature who was allowed to join them was little Kratim, the faithful dog of one of the boys.

When they got there, they began to pray, but it had been a long and difficult week, and one by one they all fell asleep, even the little dog, curled up at his master's feet. Not long after the last was asleep, the Emperor's hunting party approached, with an advance party of guards out scouring the ground to make sure that no one with rebellious ideas could threaten the Emperor. One of these guard found the cave, and the sleeping young men, whom he recognized and reported back to one of the Emperor's advisors.

The Emperor frowned when he heard this, and asked if anyone knew what these boys had decided. When told of their activity, he was further displeased. At that point the advisor began to laugh and said "My Emperor, there could be a very easy solution to this. If the boys didn't show up at court tomorrow, everyone would think they were cowards who had run away, and there would be no martyrs to draw rebels to their cause." That almost brought a smile to Decius's face as he heard the advisors idea and agreed. So the party went on, with no one the wiser, except for a few guards who lingered behind and then filled up the entrance to the cave with some of the many rocks lying nearby, so that no light and no air could come in.

Sure enough, the next day those boys did not appear, to the surprise of their fellow Christians, who thought they were true. But it was talked about for only a short while and then, like all things, it passed, and soon Decius went

*back to Rome and it was all forgotten. Then Decius him-
self was gone and there was a new emperor. Then even
Rome was no longer the capital, and it moved to Con-
stantinople, and then the Empire itself became Christian.*

*Time kept passing, and then, one day about three hun-
dred years after the Decius visit to Ephesus, a local
farmer, who had bought some new cows and was worry-
ing about where to keep them, happened to pass the pile
of rocks that had once been the opening to the cave and
had a good idea. So, the next day he, his brothers and
cousins and neighbors, all came and took those rocks
back to his farm, where they began work on a barn for
the cows.*

*The next dawn, for the first time in all those years, light
came into the cave, and gently warmed the eyes of the
young men. One by one they woke up, yawned and
looked around sheepishly at one another as they realized
that their promise of keeping vigil all night had been
broken Even little Kratim woke up, and stretched out his
little legs and shook himself into alertness.*

*All were amazed at how soundly they had slept, as if it
had been a long time. They discussed their situation.
One wanted to go down right away and face their fate,
one thought maybe they should reconsider their decision, since if they stayed alive they could carry on their
work and if they died people might forget the message.
One thought it possible that Decius would have just gone
back to Rome, having gotten bored with the boar hunt.
One, who never could forget his stomach, which felt as if
it had been empty for a week, thought that it would not
hurt anything if they at least had a decent breakfast on
this important day,. Finally it was decided that one,
Marcus, who was the smartest, would go into town. He*

would see if there was any news to affect them and bring back some nice fresh rolls for breakfast.

He went down toward town, but when he got to the gate—there was a cross over it. Wondering if it were some kind of trap, he walked around the walls to the next gate, where there was another cross. When there was still another cross at the third gate, he decided to go in anyway, and followed his nose to a bakery, since this was not a part of town he knew. The fresh bread smelled wonderful, and the line seemed very long as he waited. He noticed how strangely everyone was dressed, but paid it no mind.

Then it was his turn at the counter, and he asked for eight rolls, not forgetting the little dog. They were wrapped up and he put down his coins and started out the door. The baker called out to him, and asked where he had gotten these coins. Marcus said, "they were mine and my friends," and turned to go.

The baker was not a stupid man, though. He had seen the face on those coins, and they were not of Emperor Theodosius. They looked like some old dead Emperor, and anyone who had them must have stolen them from a hoard somewhere that would belong to the Emperor. He was not about to be accused of stealing from the Emperor, so he shouted, "Stop Thief," and jumped over the counter. Marcus started to run, and soon the whole store was after him. He hoped to find a familiar face, but knew no one and finally was stopped by the crowd. He told them how he and his friends were waiting to be tried as Christians that very day, and they looked at him blankly. He told them to call for a friend who would vouch for him, but no one had heard the name.

Finally, the bishop was called, and when he heard the story he sent someone to the cave to test the boy's story and when he found the others there he brought them back. The bishop was so astonished at the tale that he sent for the Emperor himself to come see these wondrous boys. The Emperor came, and when he heard their story wanted to declare them saints and take them to court. But they answered only that they must have been saved by God to prove his omnipotence and wanted nothing more than to be allowed to spend the rest of their days in prayer at the cave.

Reluctantly, the Emperor agreed, and the young men went to their cave again. The next morning, when someone brought them some breakfast, nothing was found but their bones. Filled with even more wonder, the Emperor wanted to put their bones in fancy reliquaries covered with precious stones, but in a dream the seven came to him and told him that they had become stars to provide constant proof of God's majesty and love.

And we can see them still, today, as the seven stars that form the constellation we call the big dipper. Seven stars, circling around the fixed star to the north. Seven stars, plus one tiny one. If you look at the top of the handle of the dipper you can see tiny Alcol, really the dog Kratim, faithful forever to his faithful master and his friends.

This story, of "The Seven Sleepers of Ephesus," is told by Christian and Muslim alike in that part of the world. That little dog is one of the few animals ever allowed into Mohammedan heaven, according to tradition. You can even find travel sites on the Internet, with pictures of what is supposed to be their graves. When I first heard about bin Laden moving to the caves in Afghanistan, I thought of this story, and wondered if he was thinking of it, too, and identifying with the heroes. It is a lovely story, and it pains me that some may view America in the role of the evil Roman empire. Story is a very powerful thing, and that power can be used for many purposes.

To close, I would like to come full circle and wish for that anonymous ironworker what Ben Okri has assured us is the outcome of real storytelling:

> *When we have made an experience or a chaos into a story we have transformed it, made sense of it, transmuted experience, domesticated chaos.*[15]

Notes

1. Anonymous. This poem was scribbled as graffiti on the sidewalk by Union Square, right after September 11, 2001. The misspelled "helld" seems a very appropriate error.

2. Samuel Taylor Coleridge (1797) *The Rime of the Ancient Mariner*. An excerpt:

> *An ancient Mariner meeteth three Gallants bidden to a wedding-feast, and detaineth one.*
>
> It is an ancient Mariner,
> And he stoppeth one of three.
> 'By thy long beard and glittering eye,
> Now wherefore stopp'st thou me ?
>
> The Bridegroom's doors are opened wide,
> And I am next of kin;
> The guests are met, the feast is set:
> May'st hear the merry din.
>
> He holds him with his skinny hand,
> 'There was a ship,' quoth he.

'Hold off ! unhand me, grey-beard loon!'
Eftsoons his hand dropt he.

The Wedding-Guest is spell-bound by the eye of the old seafaring man,
and constrained to hear his tale.

He holds him with his glittering eye–
The Wedding-Guest stood still,
And listens like a three years' child:
The Mariner hath his will.

The Wedding-Guest sat on a stone:
He cannot choose but hear;
And thus spake on that ancient man,
The bright-eyed Mariner.

3. Emily Dickinson, "A Doubt If It Be Us." (1864).

4. Roger C. Schank, *Tell Me a Story: A New Look at Real and Artificial Memory* (New York: Scribners, 1990).

5. William Shakespeare, *Henry V*. Renascence editions. Available at: www.uoregon.edu/~rbear/shake/hv.html (7 January 2002).

6. www.hereisnewyork.org (4 April 2002) 629, photographed by Adam Forgash c. 2001. The ironworker did not leave his name. A book with some of the photographs has been released; this one is on page 167. It was conceived and organized by Alice Rose George, Gilles Peress, Michael Shulan, and Charles Traub, *Here Is New York: A Democracy of Photographs* (Zurich: Scalo, 2002).

7. Walter J. Ong, *Orality and Literacy: The Technologizing of the Word* (London: Routledge, 1988 [1982]).

8. Herbert I. Schiller, *Information Inequality: The Deepening Social Crisis in America* (New York: Routledge, 1996).

9. The Rolling Stones, *Yesterday's Papers* (© 1967 Mick Jagger and Keith Richard).

10. Guy Debord, *The Society of the Spectacle* (NewYork: Black & Red, 1977 [1970]). *La Société du Spectacle.* (Paris: Editions Buchet-Chastel, 1967).

11. Guy Debord, *Comments on The Society of the Spectacle*. Translated by Malcolm Imrie (London: Verso, 1990). Available at: notbored.org/commentaires.html.

12. Donna J. Haraway, *Modest_Witness@Second_Millenium: FemaleMan(c)_Meets_OncoMouse(tm)* (New York: Routledge, 1997).

13. Ellis is co-author of a book about telling stories on painful subjects: Loren Niemi and Elizabeth Ellis. *Inviting the Wolf In: Thinking About Difficult Stories* (Little Rock, Ark.: August House, 2001).

14. Elizabeth tells this story about Scooter with his permission, and I tell this anecdote about that story with hers.

15. Ben Okri, "Aphorisms and Fragments from 'The Joys of Storytelling' " no. 22, *Birds of Heaven* (London: Phoenix, 1996).

Chapter 9

Myth in an Age of Information

Introduction to the Talk

This was originally delivered at Texas Woman's University, as the Lillian Bradshaw Lecture, Denton, Texas, April 24, 1998. It was printed privately by TWU and was published, in slightly different version, as: "Myth in an Age of Information: Can We Synthesize 'Truth' and 'Fact'?" in Journal of Youth Services in Libraries 12:2 (Winter 1999), 18-24. Reprinted with permission of the American Library Association.

The dean of Texas Woman's University's School of Library and Information Science heard about a course I had designed called Myth in the Age of Information and asked me to deliver the 1998 Lillian Bradshaw Lecture based on it. That class had grown out of my own reaction to doctoral students coming to Information Studies from divergent academic backgrounds and widely differing world views. As a storyteller, I saw that these were intellectual belief systems with their own stories about the world.

TWU's SLIS wanted to develop a Master's program in Storytelling, and hoped that a lecture on why it was important in an academic context would help convince the administration of the university that this was a good idea. It worked, and, as co-chair of the committee designing the program, I was lucky enough to work with such great storytellers as Donald Davis and Margie MacDonald. Unfortunately, the president of the university left before it went to the state legislature for approval, and the new president didn't follow through.

Myth in an Age of Information

*Space-ships and time machines are no escape from the human
condition. Let Othello subject Desdemona to a lie-detector
test; his jealousy will still blind him to the evidence. Let Oedipus triumph over gravity; he won't triumph over his fate.*

Arthur Koestler [1]

People of the modern age have prided themselves on their supe-
riority to those foolish people of earlier ages who were ruled by
silly superstition. We are rational beings, guided by reason and
intellect, not emotion. Well, yes . . . and no. Human nature has
not changed very much. We are still governed by myths—it is
just that we are no longer conscious of them as belief systems—
and that leaves us just as vulnerable to error as before. Myths are
still the best explanations for large parts of our humanness,
which can only be understood indirectly. Therefore, it is important to study both myth and its traditional form of presentation,
storytelling. The academic world in particular needs this as balance, to keep from deluding itself into the belief that humans can
be entirely rational.

This is not meant to downplay rationality or science. Far
from it. It is simply to acknowledge that we are creatures of
emotion as well as logic and cannot ask science to meet all our
need for meaning in our lives.

Rollo May spoke of this need today:

> As a practicing psychoanalyst I find that contemporary ther-
> apy is almost entirely concerned . . . with the problems of the
> individual's search for myths. The fact that Western society
> has all but lost its myths was the main reason for the birth and
> development of psychoanalysis in the first place. . . . I speak
> of the *Cry* for myths because I believe there is an urgency in
> the need for myth in our day. Many of the problems of our so-
> ciety, including cults and drug addiction, can be traced to the
> lack of myths which will give us as individuals the inner secu-
> rity we need in order to live adequately in our day.[2]

What is this "myth?" According to one expert, "myth is a 'true story,' . . . not literally, but in its implicit meaning." The basic *Webster's* definition of myth is: "A story, the origin of which is forgotten, ostensibly historical but usually such as to explain some practice, belief, institution or natural phenomenon. Myths are especially associated with religious rites and beliefs."[3]

Rollo May has given a powerful explanation. He says:

> A myth is a way of making sense in a senseless world. Myths are narrative patterns that give significance to our existence. Whether the meaning of existence is only what we put into life by our own individual fortitude, as Sartre would hold, or whether there is a meaning we need to discover, as Kierkegaard would state, the result is the same, myths are our way of finding this meaning and significance. Myths are like the beams in a house: not exposed to outside view, they are the structure which holds the house together so people can live in it.[4]

According to James Hillman, myth is "the thing you're in and don't know is a myth."[5] In other words, that which we unquestioningly assume to be the truth. So, what we have lost is the sense of myth, not myth itself. Max Muller put it this way: "Depend on it. There is mythology now as there was in the time of Homer, only we do not perceive it, because we ourselves live in the very shadow of it, and because we all shrink from the full meridian light of truth." [6]

Most people still find their sense of meaning in organized religions, but for many in the academic community and the secular world, science has become the basic belief system. When I first had this thought, it seemed very startling, but since then I have discovered from reading that many others have had the same idea. Robert Johnson, for example, says "Science is our present myth. For most people, science is their religion."[7] Edward Edinger puts it in a way that sounds more "scientific": "Science is man's current authority, the one thing that's believable."[8]

I have a book entitled *Science Is God,* that in the library of an older friend who had been haunted by having worked on the Manhattan Project developing the atomic bomb. According to the book:

> Science is the modern god. In a disturbingly large number of ways, the position of science in the mid-twentieth century parallels that of religion in the mid-nineteenth. Twentieth-century scientists, like nineteenth century theologians, make the wildest claims on behalf of their god, not realizing the danger that if these claims are proved false their god may fall. Twentieth-century charlatans of a myriad varieties offer their panaceas for society and attempt to mislead the people by calling their misbegotten concepts scientific. And bewildered twentieth-century common men have a crude faith in their god which they do not care to have questioned too closely but which could be destroyed if it were demonstrated that their graven image has feet of clay.[9]

This prediction has been coming true for some time, as some people blame science for such side effects of technology as pollution and scientists, in their turn, defend their belief system.[10] There is nothing wrong with a deep respect for science, we just cannot expect reason to fill all needs and must recognize that it seems that human beings need to depend on something beyond themselves. For many, that something is religion; for others, it may be a belief in the perfectibility of mankind or in a political system.

Technology, like fire, makes a good servant, but a bad master. To quote Albert Einstein: "We should take care not to make the intellect our god; it has, of course, powerful muscles, but no personality."[11] Archibald MacLeish puts it this way, "We are deluged with facts, but we have lost, or are losing, our human ability to feel them . . ."[12] Many people are so afraid of being ruled by emotion that they risk throwing the baby out with the bathwater and forgetting that the head and heart are supposed to work together. In an effort to disown the embarrassment of one's own childhood beliefs in almost anything, these people try to distance themselves as adults by debunking almost everything. Such an attitude misses the fact that cynicism is a kind of negative gullibility, rather than a mature evaluation of individual instances.

To return to Rollo May:

> When we in the twentieth century are so concerned about proving that our technical reason is right and we wipe away in one fell swoop the "silliness" of myths, we also rob our own souls and we threaten to destroy our society as part of the same deterioration.[13]
>
> There can be no stronger proof of the impoverishment of our contemporary culture than the popular—though profoundly mistaken—definition of myth as falsehood.[14]
>
> The denial of myths . . . is itself part of our refusal to confront our own reality and that of our society.[15]

J.B.S. Haldane, the British scientist, may have said it even better: "The wise man regulates his conduct by the theories both of religion and science. But he regards these theories not as statements of ultimate fact but as art-forms."[16]

Once again, Einstein has an appropriate thought:

> The most beautiful emotion we can experience is the mystical. It is the power of all true art and science. He to whom this emotion is a stranger, who can no longer wonder and stand rapt in awe, is as good as dead . . . this feeling, is at the center of true religiousness. In this sense, and in this sense only, I belong to the rank of devoutly religious men.[17]

Modern thinkers have trouble considering anything that smacks, even indirectly, of religion. According to one scholar of religion: "Since the Enlightenment, hatred of religion has been a more respectable scholarly emotion than love, particularly hatred for one's own religion. . . . The simultaneous use of heart and head seems to violate many of the unspoken canons of scholarship . . ."[18] She also feels that academicians are afraid of religions' power, which can result in evil as well as good, but denial of this important aspect of being human is, just as clearly, dangerous to society.

She finishes her book by saying:

> We are left, then, sometimes with no myths, sometimes with myths emasculated of their rituals, sometimes with bad myths that trap us. . . . But we may break out from all of these various prisons with the help of other peoples' myths, which, coming from outside our own closed system, may . . . move us off our own treadmill, our own track, onto an entirely new path. New myths move us into new worlds where we can begin to think thoughts that not only were impossible to think within our old familiar world of ideas but that we could not even realize we had been unable to think in that world. In this way we are sometimes able to change both our myths and our lives—or at least to give new myths to our children.[19]

Looking at this loss of myth and story from an entirely different academic perspective, that of the literary critic and theorist, Karl Kroeber says:

> . . . one of modernism's most revolutionary acts was to categorize storytelling as 'primitive,' as an activity peculiar to 'undeveloped' people either lost within or marginal to 'advanced' Western culture. In their (the Third World) stories the vital social purposes of narrative are conspicuous, and their unfamiliarity may alert us to the parochialism of our supposedly 'universal' critical principles, which often merely express the historical idiosyncrasy of those fears and needs we would sooner not acknowledge."[20]
> " . . . we must recognize that modernism's contestations of narrative are not a trivial stylistic peculiarity but a profoundly serious and unusual event in human history, both the causes and implications of which demand more thoughtful analysis than they have as yet received."[21]

So, among the ranks of psychologists, physicists, physiologists, philologists and philosophers, to say nothing of religious historians, poets and literary experts, are people concerned about the loss of myth in modern society. But it is not only scientists who have found new things to believe in, and not only scholars who have noticed the common lack of belief systems and the hunger that humankind seems to be feeling.

I suspect that a large portion of our society puts real faith in the power of money. That is a whole different topic, but what about consumer society? What about Madison Avenue? Sal Randazzo, author of *Mythmaking on Madison Avenue*, says:

> Advertising is a storied form of communication, a narrative fiction, that in addition to communicating information about the product, tries to reflect the values, lifestyles and sensibilities of the target consumer and/or culture. . . . Every brand tells a story about itself. And people get to know the brands through the stories they tell in much the same way people get to know each other—by each one relating one's own life story to the other. [22]

Popular culture has jumped in with both feet. What about all those fantasy games and video games peopled with fantastic creatures? Just look at all the television programs based on standard figures that often appear in myths. What about all the cartoon tricksters and the unceasing vying for dominance between Tom and Jerry or Roadrunner and Coyote? What could be said about Dilbert and the other cynical heroes who humorously reflect the modern despair of those in jobs they find meaningless?

Hollywood is quite conscious of being in the business of making myths. According to *Star Myths: Show Business Biographies on Film:*

> A myth is not a lie. Although many people confuse the terms, there is a very important difference between them. Lies are instantaneous, they occur whenever one person tries to deceive another. Myths are ancient; they represent not humanities pitiful attempts at deception, but the age-old struggle to understand and fit life into ordered predictable, comprehensible pat-

terns of events—patterns which then allow the mind to perceive a kind of pre-scientific meaning or answer to the riddle
of existence. Myths function as the basis for all storytelling,
but captured in this delimited linear state, they can be put to all
sorts of uses both noble and ignoble. [23]

The whole world of business has awakened to storytelling and
myth as management technique as well as marketing ploy. A few
recent book titles show this: *Managing by Storying Around*; [24]
and *Corporate Legends and Lore: The Power of Storytelling as a
Management Tool*; [25] to say nothing of the whole new field of
scenario-building based on Peter Schwartz's *The Long View* [26]
and his Global Business Network. This is a management technique for planning, based on designing strategies by telling stories, called scenarios, about possible futures and then using these
to make choices, taking likely eventualities into account. As
Wendell Bell says of Future Studies: "The primary goal of futurists is not to predict the future, but to uncover images of possible,
probable, and preferable futures that enable people to make in-
formed decisions about their lives." [27] As another futurologist
puts it: "The best way to predict the future is to invent it." [28]
Well, well, well, here we are back at delphic oracles, just more
scientific than religious ones.

In other words, we are a part of a mythic culture, simply by being human. And, as has been said in other contexts, if we don't
take charge of our own lives, someone else will happily do so for
us. The choice is to try to make sense of this all for ourselves. As
Rollo May put it:

> Every individual seeks—indeed *must* seek if he or she is to
> remain sane—to bring some order and coherence into the
> stream of sensations, emotions, and ideas entering his or her
> consciousness from within or without. Each one of us is forced
> to do deliberately for oneself what in previous ages was done
> by family, custom, church and state, namely, form the myths
> in terms of which we can make some sense of experience. [29]

"Myths permeate all areas of modern life,"[30] says David:

> Now we find an abundance of mortal heroes and heroines, both real and imaginary, in novels, comics, movies and television stories. While these images are less than venerable—rather than reaching back through the generations, they appear suddenly and fade abruptly—they are disseminated through powerful media and leave strong impressions. The lyrics of popular songs often provide compelling mythic messages that may later appear word for word in a teenager's protestation of love, statement of defiance, or suicide note.[31]

> Cultural myths have been drifting toward obsolescence more swiftly since the midcentury than in any previous period of history. The half-life of a valid guiding myth has never been briefer, and we see new myths being hammered out daily on the anvil of people's lives . . .[32] Guiding myths that were workable in recent memory have lost their viability at a dizzying pace. As history has advanced more rapidly, so has the need to become more facile in revising the myths that guide us.[33]

The poet Robert Bly, with his *Iron John*, represents the perspective of the new age community of people who are trying to take charge of their own myths and designing ones to fit current needs. He says:

> We are living at an important and fruitful moment now, for it is clear to men that the images of adult manhood given by the popular culture are worn out; a man can no longer depend on them. By the time a man is thirty-five he knows that the images of the right man, the tough man, the true man which he received in high school do not work in life. Such a man is open to new visions of what a man is or could be.

> The hearth and fairy stories have passed, as water through fifty feet of soil, through generations of men and women, and we can trust their images more than, say, those invented by HC Andersen. The images the old stories give—stealing the key from under the mother's pillow, picking up a golden feather

fallen from the burning breast of the Firebird, finding the Wild
Man under the lake water, following the tracks of one's own
wound through the forest and finding that it resembles the
tracks of a god—these are meant to be taken slowly into the
body. They continue to unfold, once taken in.[34]

Later, he says:

> The grief in men has been increasing steadily since the start of
> the Industrial Revolution and the grief has reached a depth
> now that cannot be ignored.

> The dark side of men is clear. Their mad exploitation of earth
> resources, devaluation and humiliation of women, and obses-
> sion with tribal warfare are undeniable. Genetic inheritance
> contributes to their obsessions, but also culture and environ-
> ment; we have defective mythologies that ignore masculine
> depth of feeling, assign men a place in the sky instead of earth,
> teach obedience to the wrong powers, work to keep men boys,
> and entangle both men and women in systems of industrial
> domination that exclude both matriarchy and patriarchy.[35]

Another person working with myths for the modern world is
psychotherapist Stephen Larsen who studied with Joseph Campbell. He says:

> I believe that the mythic revival that is now under way is no
> mere fad. In modern times myths have been thought of as illu-
> sions, but if so, they are the kind that still retain the power, as
> Joseph Campbell put it: "to carry the human spirit forward."
> Psychologist Jean Houston identified myth as the cognitive
> and emotional DNA of the psyche—somehow ever new, al-
> ways generative, yet as old as the hills that hide the ancient se-
> crets of our race.

> The fresh and open mind of the child creates and understands
> myths intuitively, whereas the psychotherapist, the creative
> writer, and the scholar labor long to mine myth's rich veins of
> wisdom and creative inspiration. Yet even now, mythology
> emerges as the legacy of a whole planet. To understand other

people and other cultures and the images we share—and fail to share—with our fellows, we must relearn an aboriginal language; the universal tongue of the human imagination. With its inexhaustible vocabulary of symbol and story, it is at once our ancestral birthright and the ever-brimming well of dreams into which we look to find our future. I call this innate resource of ours "the mythic imagination."[36]

So much for the present; and what of the future? Mechanical engineer J.G. Falcioni compares the industrial revolution and its "machines that changed raw materials into physical products . . . applying physical leverage, a multiplier for the power of human muscle" with the current information revolution in which we are developing "intellectual leverage, a multiplier for the human mind."[37] We are in a time of major change, on many fronts. Maria-Therese Hoppe, Director of Research for the Copenhagen Institute for Future Studies takes it to the next stage. She says that in the future we will all need powerful imaginations to cope with the pace of change. Then, dreamers will be prized just as those who can skillfully manipulate data are prized now.[38]

Ah, yes—this reminds me of the old prediction of Irish storyteller Padraic Colum:

> Some time, perhaps soon, it will come to be recognized that it is as important to cultivate the imagination as it is to cultivate the will or the intelligence. . . . For imagination is one of the great faculties; it is the one faculty common to all exceptional people—to soldiers, statesmen, saints; to artists, scientists, philosophers and great businessmen. Says the Serpent to Eve in "Back to Methuselah," "She told it to me as a marvelous story of something that never happened to a Lilith that never was. She did not know that imagination is the beginning of creation. You imagine what you desire; you will what you imagine; and at last you create what you will." The day may come when that sentence will be written above all places of education: "Imagination is the beginning of creation. You imagine what you desire; you will what you imagine; and at last you create what you will."[39]

Or, to go back to Albert Einstein, one last time, "imagination is more important than knowledge." Indeed, the story is told (from storyteller to storyteller) that, when he was asked how to become a great scientist, he answered "read fairy tales." When that answer did not satisfy the questioner, who persisted, "what else?" he replied "read more fairy tales."

Good advice.

I believe it is important that people who care about society study myth as literature and storytelling as a process, not as means to the end of manipulating people into buying objects or buying into cults, but to open listeners into seeing their humanness in a way that is not frightening or demeaning, but, rather, full of meaning, as well as adventure, fun and the enchantment of truths.

We have been talking about myths, and the tone has been fairly heavy but stories for entertainment and plain old escape are also of great value, building imaginations with courage, compassion and respect, with humor and joy. I enter a plea that we give our children the raw material for building their own futures, their own wisdom, by telling them stories and encouraging them to do the same.

Notes

1. Arthur Koestler, "The Boredom of Fantasy," pt. 2, in *The Trail of the Dinosaur and Other Essays* (London: Collins, 1955 [1953]).

2. Rollo May, foreword, *The Cry for Myth* (New York: Delta Books, 1992) [1991], 9.

3. *Webster's Collegiate Dictionary* 5th ed., s.v. "myth."

4. May, *The Cry for Myth*, 15.

5. James Hillman, quoted in: "Inheritance of Dreams," vol. 2. *The Wisdom of the Dream: Carl Gustav Jung* (video) (RM assoc. Stephen Segaller Films, 1989). Alfred Adler spoke often of how humans all worked from a "guiding fiction."

6. Max Muller, "The Philosophy of Mythology," *The Science of Religion* (London: Longmans Green, 1873), 353-355. Quoted in: May, *The Cry for Myth*, 25.

7. Robert Johnson, quoted in: "Inheritance of Dreams." vol. 2. *The Wisdom of the Dream: Carl Gustav Jung.* (video) (RM assoc. Stephen Segaller Films. 1989).

8. Edward F. Edinger, quoted in: "Inheritance of Dreams." vol. 2. *The Wisdom of the Dream: Carl Gustav Jung.* (video) (RM assoc. Stephen Segaller Films. 1989).

9. David F. Horrobin, *Science Is God* (Aylesbury, England: Medical and Technical Publishing Co. Ltd., 1969), 163.

10. For example, Martin Luther King Jr. felt that "We have genuflected before the god of science only to find that it has given us the atomic bomb, producing fears and anxieties that science can never mitigate," Chapter 13. *Strength To Love* (New York: Harper & Row, 1963). And, just in case anyone really believes that scientists are always dispassionate, Carl Sagan proved his humanity by lashing out at those who turn apostate in: Carl Sagan, *The Demon-Haunted World: Science as a Candle in the Dark* (New York: Random House, 1995).

11. Albert Einstein, Chapter 51. *Out of My Later Years* (New York: Philosophical Library, 1950).

12. Archibald MacLeish, "Poetry and Journalism," *A Continuing Journey* (Boston: Houghton Mifflin, 1967), 43. Quoted in May, *The Cry for Myth*, 23.

13. May, *The Cry for Myth*, 19.

14. May, *The Cry for Myth*, 23.

15. May, *The Cry for Myth*, 25.

16. J.B.S. Haldane. "Science and Theology as Art-Forms," *Possible Worlds, and other Papers* (Freeport, N.Y.: Books for Libraries Press, 1971). Originally published as *Possible Worlds and Other Essays* (London: Chatto & Windus, 1927). Jung called this the "psychological vertigo of living without a myth." Carl Gustav Jung, foreword to *Symbols of Transformation*, 2nd ed. Bollingen Series 20, vol 5. (Princeton, N.J.: Princeton University Press, 1967 [1912]), xxv. Quoted in Stephen Larsen, *The Mythic Imagination* (see note 44), 13.

17. Albert Einstein, Quoted in: Philipp Frank, *Einstein: His Life and Times*, chapter 12, section 5, translated by George Rosen (New York: A.A. Knopf, 1947).

18. O'Flaherty, *Other People's Myths*, 18.

19. O'Flaherty, *Other People's Myths*, 165-166.

20. Karl Kroeber, *Retelling/Rereading: The Fate of Storytelling in Modern Times* (New Brunswick, N.J.: Rutgers University Press, 1992), 4.

21. Karl Kroeber, *Retelling/Rereading*, 85.

22. Sal Randazzo, *Mythmaking on Madison Avenue* (Chicago, Ill.: Probus, 1993).

23. Robert Milton Miller, *Star Myths: Show Business Biographies on Film* (Metuchen, N.J.: Scarecrow Press, 1983), ix.

24. David Armstrong, *Managing by Storying Around: A New Method of Leadership* (New York: Currency/Doubleday 1992).

25. Peg Neuhauser, *Corporate Legends and Lore: The Power of Storytelling as a Management Tool* (New York: McGraw-Hill, 1993).

26. Peter Schwartz, *The Long View: Scenario Building* (New York: Currency/Doubleday, 1996 [1991]).

27. Wendell Bell, *Foundations of Futures Studies* (Transaction, 1997). Quoted in "The Purposes of Futures Studies," *The Futurist* 31 no. 6 (November-December 1997).

28. Peter Cochrane of British Petroleum was quoted as saying this in an article on futurology in *The European,* 23 February-1 March, 1998, 30-31.

29. May, *The Cry for Myth*, 29.

30. David Feinstein and Stanley Krippner, *Personal Mythology: The Psychology of Your Evolving Self* (Los Angeles, Calif.: Targer/Perigee, 1988), 5.

31. Feinstein and Krippner, *Personal Mythology*, 5.

32. Feinstein and Krippner, *Personal Mythology*, 6. He seems to be using "myth" in the way that François Lyotard used "metanarrative."

33. Feinstein and Krippner, *Personal Mythology*, 7.

34. Robert Bly, *Iron John: A Book about Men* (New York: Vintage/Random House, 1992), ix.

35. Bly, *Iron John*, x.

36. Stephen Larsen, Introduction. *The Mythic Imagination: The Quest for Meaning through Personal Mythology* (Rochester, Vt.: Inner Traditions, 1996), xvii-xviii.

37. J. G. Falcioni, "Preparing for the Next Revolution," *Mechanical Engineering,* 119 no. 3 (New York: M. Dekker, 1997), 4.

38. Maria-Therese Hoppe was quoted as saying this in an article on futurology in *The European,* (23 February - 1 March, 1998), 30-31.

39. Padraic Colum, "Storytelling, New and Old," in *Fountains of Youth* (New York: Macmillan, 1940 [1927]), 193-206.

Chapter 10

Conclusion:

Story as Social Glue

Introduction to the Talk

This chapter, like the first one, was written for the book, so you, as reader, must be the only audience. I hope you have enjoyed the book, and found yourself thinking about it and that you carry the thought on to other "hearers," whether in spoken or written form—but most of all I hope that you become a storyteller, whether a formal one or, more naturally, in your everyday life.

Conclusion:

Story as Social Glue

". . . scientific knowledge does not represent the totality of knowledge; it has always existed in addition to, and in competition and conflict with, another kind of knowledge, which I will call narrative. . . . I do not mean to say that narrative knowledge can prevail over science, but its model is related to ideas of internal equilibrium and conviviality next to which contemporary scientific knowledge cuts a poor figure, especially if it is to undergo an exteriorization with respect to the "knower" and an alienation from its user even greater than has previously been the case."

François Lyotard[1]

These talks were all intended to encourage their hearers to consider the place of story in our world and storytelling as a means of counteracting some of the artificiality of our current culture. It should be possible for each of us to step back far enough to gain a perspective that includes Lyotard's scientific and narrative knowledges, both. As thoughts and speculations, these talks have been meant to provoke others into combining both types of thinking and developing new ideas.

Manuel Castells has expressed the conviction that the struggle of the information age lies between the individual and the net (i.e., the interwoven net of information to which we are but data).[2] If he is right, then the ability to maintain our perception of ourselves in terms of story as well as facts may be very important factor in how well we survive as human beings in the midst of the techno-world we have constructed. It may also be a major factor in how we negotiate with the parts of humanity who are not part of that world but linger in the narrative knowledges described by Lyotard.

These talks were not been meant to be a condemnation of all technology—which would be pretty stupid, since that is our reality and not likely to change because of a few Cassandras crying in the techno-wilderness. I agree with John Steinbeck, when he said:

. . . I run into people who seem to feel that literature is all words and that those words should preferably be a little stuffy. Who knows what literature is? The literature of the Cro Magnon is painted on the walls of the caves of Altamira. Who knows but that the literature of the future will be projected on clouds. Our present argument that literature is the written and printed word in poetry, drama and the novel has no very eternal basis in fact. Such literature has not been with us very long, and there is nothing to indicate that it will continue with us for very long (at least the way it is going). If people don't read it, it just isn't going to be literature.[3]

Steinbeck wrote this, about the work of the cartoonist Al Capp, in 1953. Although there were fears even then that film would replace the book entirely, it has not disappeared. The point is that new circumstances will cause the creation of new forms; I share Steinbeck's hopes of wonderful new media and enjoy the electronic ones of today as much as the older ones on canvas or paper.

At the same time, we must be responsible to ourselves and to the future, by considering what the impact of all this is, and try to maintain what is essential from traditional forms. We must be sure that forms and materials of value are not being lost in the glamour of the new and glittering

The psychologist and philosopher May fears that we are losing much by abandoning old myths. He compares us to ancient Greece. Early on, people had myths to make sense of their world without guilt or anxiety and philosophers had the luxury of attending to beauty, truth, goodness, and courage. Later, when society had become more sophisticated, according to Lucretius Greece was a place of "aching hearts in every home, racked incessantly by pangs the mind was powerless assuage and forced to vent themselves in recalcitrant repining."[4] May compares this to our search for psychotherapy, drugs, and cults to hold anxiety and guilt at bay, and quotes Jerome Bruner, "For when the prevailing myths fail to fit the varieties of man's plight, frustration expresses itself first in mythoclasm [i.e., the destruction of myths] and then in the lonely search for internal identity."[5]

That sounds pretty melodramatic, but it is worth at least some attention. In order to prevent that loss and the accompanying unhappiness, it is necessary to consider the old forms and maintain them at least until their role is understood. Researchers in information need to understand story, its power and its peculiarities. Clearly the time has come to do this. In the time since I gave the first of these speeches, some people are beginning to try to study and understand it, while others try to exploit it as another tool in controlling information and a few others try to exploit the consumers of that product.

If any readers with a research bent have made it this far, it is to be hoped that they will work to enhance story's role. It is also to be hoped that people interested in story itself, rather than as part of the information world, will be encouraged to think about its larger impact beyond the particular tale or time of telling.

The introduction to this book included a parable from McLuhan and an anecdote about my mother. I choose to end the same way. McLuhan's parable was about how we are like the fish that has no concept of water or the fact that it lives in water. He related it to the omnipresence of media, which we tend to accept without consideration and I related it to the omnipresence of story. The parable I want to connect that modern one with is an old one from India:

> There was once a poor ferryman who earned his living by carrying people across the Ganges in his little boat. One day, in spite of an approaching storm, three important people demanded that he take them across. He could not afford to lose the business and so he agreed, though reluctantly.
>
> The three passengers spent time bragging. One was wealthy, one learned and one a well-known musician. Having impressed each other, one of them turned to the ferryman and asked what important books he had read.
>
> "I am a humble waterman, who cannot read or write," he admitted.
>
> "Then you have wasted half your life," said the scholar condescendingly.

The next man then asked what instrument he could play.

"I am a humble waterman, who cannot play any musical instruments," he admitted.

The response came: "You have wasted at least a quarter of your life, then."

Finally the rich man asked about his wealth.

"I am a humble waterman, who can earn only a little rowing people across the river," he admitted.

"Well, said the wealthy man: "You have wasted half your life then, with no wealth to show for your work."

The ferryman was working hard, and they were almost across the wide river, but the weather was so bad that the boat was swamped with water and could not make it the rest of the way. The ferryman told them that they were lucky enough to be close to the shore so that they could swim to safety.

"But I can't swim!" said the three important men, in unison.

"Then your whole lives are wasted," called the ferryman as he jumped into the river and swam to safety.

I suggest that storytelling and understanding stories is like swimming, a humble art, but one that is necessary for survival in our technological world as much as any other. Our consciousness still swims in an ocean of story, even if it is mediated through technology.

An anecdote about my mother gives this chapter its title. She played hostess to a group of student writers that my father advised and would stay to hear people read their work. Her favorite was a poem written by a student from Japan. It was an ode to the role of women, and ended up in praise of "woman, mother, social glue." She knew from a Japanese artist friend that glue is a respected substance, but had never considered it in a social context and the unexpected phrase struck her as funny and she had to suppress the urge to laugh.

For the rest of her life, whenever a woman had managed to resolve some difficulty, she would quote that: ". . . woman, mother, social glue." I ask that you consider the way that story too, is a form of social glue—worthy of respect even as we take it for granted. To use another domestic analogy, it interweaves through our lives, simultaneously connecting the warp and woof of familiar and unexpected perspectives to create a living tapestry from fragments of thread.

I remember, as a teenager being struck with the thought that "truth is a jewel with many facets." The recognition was a big one, even as I knew that my phrase was embarrassingly pompous and must have been thought by others before me. It remains true whether one is looking out at the world through a single point of view or looking from the outside and recognizing truth in a single instant of experiencing beauty or love or awe. Story is one of the best ways to learn how to see both out and in and to recognize how things are woven together and thus gain a perspective able to deal with life. Furthermore, it helps to develop a strong sense of wonder, and in the words of an old Greek proverb:

Wonder is the beginning of wisdom.

Notes

1. Lyotard, Jean-François, *The Postmodern Condition: A Report on Knowledge.* Translation from the French by Geoff Bennington and Brian Massumi (Minneapolis, Minn.: University of Minnesota Press, 1983). *La Condition postmoderne: rapport sur le savoir.* (1979) 7.

2. Castells, Manuel. The Rise of the Network Society. vol. 1 in *The Information Age: Economy, Society and Culture.*

3. Al Capp, *The World of L'il Abner,* with an introduction by John Steinbeck and a foreword by Charles Chaplin (New York: Farrar, Straus and Young, 1953), viii.

4. Lucretius, *The Nature of the Universe* (London: Penguin Books, 1951), 217. Quoted in May, *The Cry for Myth*, 16. Since this quote was taken out of context, it seems important to mention that Lucretius (Roman poet and philosopher 96-55 BC) was very much opposed to "superstition."

5. Jerome S. Bruner, "Myth and Identity" in *Myth and Myth-making*. Edited by Henry A. Murray (New York: George Braziller, 1960), 285.

BIBLIOGRAPHY

Arendt, Hannah. *Men in Dark Times*. New York: Harcourt, Brace and World, 1968.

Armstrong, David. Managing by Storying Around: A New Method of Leadership. New York: Currency/Doubleday, 1992.

Ausubel, Nathan. *A Treasury of Jewish Folktales*. New York: Galahad, 1993.

Beier, Ulli, ed. The Origin of Life and Death: African Creation Myths. London: Heinemann, 1966.

Bell, Wendell. *Foundations of Futures Studies*. New Brunswick, N.J.: Transaction, 1997.

Benjamin, Walter. *Illuminations*. Edited with introduction by Hannah Arendt. Translated by Harry Zohn. New York: Harcourt, Brace & World, 1968 [1936].

Bennett, William. The Book of Virtues: A Treasury of Great Moral Stories. New York: Simon & Schuster, 1993.

Bettelheim, Bruno. The Uses of Enchantment: The Meaning and Importance of Fairy Tales. New York: Knopf, 1976.

Bialik, Hayim Nahman, and Yehoshua Hana Ravnitzky, eds. *The Book of Legends Sefer Ha-Aggadah: Legends from the Talmud and Midrash*. Translated by William G. Braude. New York: Schocken, 1992.

Birch, Carol L., and Melissa A Heckler. *Who Says?: Essays on Pivotal Issues in Contemporary Storytelling*. Little Rock, Ark.: August House, 1996.

Birkerts, Sven. The Gutenberg Elegies: The Fate of Reading in
    an Electronic Age. New York: Fawcett/Columbine, 1994
    [1991].

Birkerts, Sven. "The Secret Life of Children." *School Library
    Journal* 45, no. 9 (September, 1999), 141-143.

Bly, Robert. *Iron John: A Book about Men.* New York: Vin-
    tage/Random House, 1992.

Brown, John Seely, A. Collins, and Paul Duguid. "Situated Cog-
    nition and the Culture of Learning." *Educational Technology*
    18 no. 1 (January/February 1989).

Brown, John Seely and Paul Dugiud. *The Social Life of Informa
    tion.* Boston: Harvard Business School Press, 2000.

Bruner, Jerome S. "Myth and Identity," in *Myth and Myth-
    making.* Ed. by Henry A. Murray. NewYork: George Brazil-
    ler, 1960.

Card, Orson Scott. *Ender's Game.* Rev. ed. New York: Tor,
    1991 [1977].

Coleridge, Samuel Taylor. *The Rime of the Ancient Mariner*,
    [1797].

Coles, Robert. *The Call of Stories: Teaching and the Moral
    Imagination.* Boston: Houghton Mifflin, 1989.

Colum, Padraic. "Storytelling, New and Old," in *Fountains of
    Youth.* New York: Macmillan, 1940 [1927].

Cowper, William. "The Task," [1785].

Crane, Stephen. "The Wayfarer," [1899].

Crawford, Walter and Michael Gorman. *Future Libraries:
    Dreams, Madness and Reality.* Chicago: American Library
    Association, 1995.

Darwin, Charles. *Descent of Man.* [1871]. Available at:
    <ftp://ibiblio.org/pub/docs/books/gutenberg/etext00/dscmn1
    0.txt>. (5 June 2002).

Day, Ronald E. "The 'Conduit Metaphor' and The Nature and
    Politics of Information Studies," *Journal of the American
    Society for Information Science* 51 no. 9 (July 2000).

Debord, Guy. *Comments on the Society of the Spectacle.* Trans-
    lated by Malcolm Imrie. London: Verso, 1990. Available at:
    www.notbored.org/commentaires.html (5 January 2002).

Debord, Guy. *The Society of the Spectacle*. New York: Black & Red, 1970. rev. 1977. *La Société du Spectacle*. Paris: Editions Buchet-Chastel, 1967.

Denning, Stephen. *The Springboard: How Storytelling Ignites Action in Knowledge-Era Organizations*. Oxford: Butterworth/Heinemann, 2001.

Dickinson, Emily. "A Doubt If It Be Us." [1864].

Egan, Kieran. Teaching as Story Telling: An Alternative Approach to Teaching and Curriculum in the Elementary School. Chicago: University of Chicago Press, 1988 [1986] Available at: www.educ.sfu.ca/people/faculty/kegan/Supplement1.html (7 July 2002).

Einstein, Albert. *Out of My Later Years*. New York: Philosophical Library, 1950.

Eliot, T.S. *The Rock*. [1934].

Ellis, Elizabeth. (CD) *Mothers and Daughters, Daughters and Mothers*. Dallas, Tex.: New Moon Productions 2001.

Falcioni, J.G. "Preparing for the Next Revolution." *Mechanical Engineering* 119 no. 3. New York: M. Dekker, 1997.

Frank, Philipp. *Einstein: His Life and Times*. Translated by George Rosen. New York: A.A. Knopf, 1947.

Feinstein, David, and Stanley Krippner. *Personal Mythology: The Psychology of Your Evolving Self*. Los Angeles, Calif.: Targer/Perigee, 1988.

Frankl, Viktor E. *Man's Search for Meaning: an Introduction to Logotherapy*. 3rd ed. New York: Touchstone/Simon & Schuster, 1984.

George, Alice Rose, Gilles Peress, Michael Shulan, and Charles Traub, *Here Is New York: A Democracy of Photographs*. Zurich, Berlin, and New York: Scalo, 2002.

Gerson, Mary-Joan. *Why the Sky Is Far Away: A Folktale from Nigeria*. Illustrated by Hope Meryman. New York: Harcourt, 1974. Also, *Why the Sky Is Far Away: A Nigerian Folktal*, illustrated by Carla Golembe. Boston: Little Brown, 1992.

Gillard, Marni. *Storyteller, Storyteacher*. York, Me.: Stenhouse, 1996.

Gorman, Michael. The Enduring Library: Technology, Tradition and the Quest for Balance. Chicago: American Library Association, 2003.

Gorman, Michael. Our Enduring Values: Librarianship in the Twenty-First Century. Chicago: American Library Association, 2000.

Gorman, Michael, and Paul Winkler. *Anglo-American Cataloging Rules, Second Revised Edition.* Chicago: American Library Association, 1998.

Greene, Graham. *The Lost Childhood and Other Essays* New York: Lothrop, Lee and Shepard, 1951.

Greene, Graham. *The Power and the Glory,* Harmondsworth, England: Penguin, 1940.

Haldane, J.B.S. "Science and Theology as Art-Forms," In *Possible Worlds, and Other Papers*. Freeport, N.Y.: Books for Libraries Press, 1971. Originally published as *Possible Worlds and Other Essays.* London: Chatto & Windus, 1927.

Haraway, Donna J. *Modest_Witness@Second_Millenium. FemaleMan © _Meets_Oncomouse* TM. *New York: Routledge, 1997.*

Hayakawa, Samuel Ichiye. *Language in Thought and Action.* New York: Harcourt Brace, 1971.

Holdaway, Don. *The Foundations of Literacy.* Portsmouth, N.H.: Heineman, 1979.

Horrobin, David F. *Science Is God.* Aylesbury, England: Medical and Technical Publishing Co. Ltd., 1969.

Huxley, Aldous. Texts and Pretexts: an Anthology with Commentaries. London Chatto & Windus 1932.

[Ironworker]. Photograph by Adam Forgash, 2001. Available at: www.hereisnewyork.org #629. Also in: Alice Rose George, Gilles Peress, Michael Shulan, and Charles Traub, eds. *Here Is New York: A Democracy of Photographs* Zurich, Berlin, and New York: Scalo, 2002.

Iser, Wolfgang. *The Act of Reading: A Theory of Response.* Baltimore, Md.: Johns Hopkins University Press, 1978.

Jensen, Rolf. The Dream Society: How the Coming Shift from Information to Imagination will Transform Your Business. New York: McGraw-Hill, 1999.

Jung, Carl Gustav. Foreword. *Symbols of Transformation.* 2nd ed. Bollingen Series 20, vol 5. Princeton, N.J.: Princeton University Press, 1967 [1912]. xxv.

[Jung] "Inheritance of Dreams." Vol. 2. *The Wisdom of the Dream: Carl Gustav Jung.* (video) RM assoc. Stephen Segaller Films. 1989.

Kennedy, John F. Commencement address, 11 June 1962, Yale University, New Haven, Conn..

Kinder, Marsha. Playing with Power in Movies, Television, and Video Games: From Muppet Babies to Teenage Mutant Ninja Turtles. Berkeley, Calif.: University of California Press, 1991.

King, Martin Luther, Jr. *Strength To Love.* New York: Harper & Row, 1963.

Koestler, Arthur. The Trail of the Dinosaur and Other Essays. London: Collins, 1955.

Kroeber, Karl. *Retelling/Rereading: the Fate of Storytelling in Modern Times.* New Brunswick, N.J.: Rutgers University Press, 1992.

Kurtz, Howard. Spin Cycle: Inside the Clinton Propaganda Machine. New York: Free Press, 1998.

Larsen, Stephen. The Mythic Imagination: The Quest for Meaning Through Personal Mythology. Rochester, Vt.: Inner Traditions, 1996.

LeBoeuf, Michael. Imagineering: How to Profit from Your Creative Powers. New York: Berkeley, 1986 [1980].

Le Guin, Ursula. *The Language of the Night.* New York: Berkeley, 1985 [1979].

Lessig, Lawrence. *Code and Other Laws of Cyberspace.* New York: Basic, 1999.

Lester, Julius. *Black Folk Tales.* illustrated by Tom Feelings. New York: Baron, 1969.

Lewis, Thomas, Fari Amini, and Richard Lannon. *A General Theory of Love.* New York: Vintage, 2000.

Locke, John. Why We Don't Talk to Each Other Anymore: The De-Voicing of Society. New York: Touchstone/Simon & Schuster, 1998.

Lucretius (96-55 BC). *The Nature of the Universe*. London: Penguin Books, 1951.

Luthi, Max. *Once Upon a Time: On the Nature of Fairy Tales*. New York: Ungar, 1970.

Lyotard, Jean François. *The Postmodern Condition: A Report on Knowledge*. Paris: Report to the French Government, 1979. Translation from the French by Geoff Bennington and Brian Massumi. University of Minnesota Press, (n.d.).

McCarthy, Bernice. *The 4MAT System: Teaching to Learning Styles withRight/Left Mode Techniques*. Wauconda, Ill.: About Learning, Inc., 1987 [1981].

MacDonald, George. "The Fantastic Imagination," from *A Dish of Orts*. Reprint. Whitethorn, Calif.: Johannesen, 1996 [1893]. Available at: <http://www.gmsociety.org.uk/> (28 September 2002).

McLuhan, Marshall. *Understanding Media: The Extensions of Man*. New York: McGraw-Hill, 1964.

May, Rollo. *The Cry for Myth*. New York: Delta 1992 [1991].

Mellon, Nancy. *Storytelling and the Art of the Imagination*. Rockport, Mass.: Element, 1992.

Miller, Robert Milton. *Star Myths: Show Business Biographies on Film*. Metuchen, N.J.: The Scarecrow Press, 1983.

Muller, Max. "The Philosophy of Mythology." *The Science of Religion*. London: Longmans Green, 1873.

NCTE. *A Position Statement from the Committee on Storytelling National Council of Teachers of English*. Available at: <http://www.ncte.org/positions/teaching_storytelling.html> (5 May 2002).

Niemi, Loren, and Elizabeth Ellis. *Inviting the Wolf In: Thinking about Difficult Stories*. Little Rock, Ark.: August House, 2001.

Neuhauser, Peg. Corporate Legends and Lore: The Power of Storytelling as a Management Tool. New York: McGraw-Hill, 1993.

Nørretranders, Tor. *The User Illusion: Cutting Consciousness Down to Size*. Translated by Jonathan Sydenham. New York: Viking, 1998 [1991].

O'Flaherty, Wendy Doniger. *Other People's Myths: The Cave of Echoes.* New York: Macmillan, 1988.

Okri, Ben. "Aphorisms and Fragments from 'The Joys of Storytelling' " *Birds of Heaven.* London: Phoenix, 1996.

Ong, Walter. *Orality and Literacy: The Technologizing of the Word.* London and New York: Routledge, 1988 [1982].

Orwell, George. *Animal Farm.* New York: Harcourt, Brace, 1946.

Petress, Kenneth C. "Listening: A Vital Skill." *Journal of Instructional Psychology* 26 no.14 (1999), 261-262.

Pine, Joseph B. II, and James H. Gilmore. *The Experience Economy: Work Is Theatre & Every Business a Stage* (Boston, Mass.: Harvard Business School Press, 1999.

Pinker, Steven. *How the Mind Works.* New York: W.W. Norton, 1997.

MacLeish, Archibald. "Poetry and Journalism," *A Continuing Journey.* Boston: Houghton Mifflin, 1967.

Plato. *Phaedrus.* Fowler translation. Available at: www.plato.evansville.edu/texts/fowler/phaedrus14.htm (10 January 2000).

Postman, Neil. Amusing Ourselves to Death: Public Discourse in the Age of Show Business. New York: Viking, 1985.

Putnam, Robert. Bowling Alone: The Collapse and Revival of American Community. New York: Touchstone, 2001 [2000].

Randazzo, Sal. *Mythmaking on Madison Avenue.* Chicago, Ill.: Probus, 1993.

Reddy, M. J. "The Conduit Metaphor—A Case of Frame Conflict in Our Language about Language." *Metaphor and Thought*, 2nd. ed. Cambridge: Cambridge University Press, 1993, 164-201.

Reyher, Becky. *My Mother Is the Most Beautiful Woman in the World.* New York: Lothrop, Lee & Shepard, 1945.

Rodari, Gianni. *Grammatica della fantasia (Grammar of Imagination).* Turin, Italy: 1973. As translated by the Royal Danish Ministry of Foreign Affairs in their "The Power of Culture: The cultural dimension in development." © 2000. Available at: www.um.dk/danida/tpoc/chapter_3/3.5.asp. (5 May 2002).

Roe, Emery. *Narrative Policy Analysis: Theory and Practice.* Durham, N.C.: Duke University Press, 1994.

Sagan, Carl. The Demon-Haunted World: Science as a Candle in the Dark. New York: Random House, 1995.

Santillana, Giorgio de, and Hertha von Dechend, Hamlet's Mill: An Essay Investigating the Origins of Human Knowledge and Its Transmission Through Myth. Boston, Mass.: Godine, 1977 [1969].

Schank, Roger C. *Tell Me a Story: A New Look at Real and Artificial Memory.* New York: Scribners, 1990.

Schiller, Herbert I. Information Inequality: The Deepening Social Crisis in America. New York: Routledge, 1996.

Schliesman, Megan. "Talking with . . . Naomi Shihab Nye: People! People! My Heart Cried Out," *Book Links* 7 no 6. (July 1998), 38-40.

Schwartz, Peter. *The Long View: Scenario Building* NewYork: Currency/Doubleday, 1996 [1991].

Scieszka, Jon. *The True Story of the Three Little Pigs.* Pictures by Lane Smith. New York: Viking, 1989.

Shakespeare, William. *Henry V.* Renascence editions. Available at: www.uoregon.edu/~rbear/shake/hv.html (7 January 2002).

Stallings, Fran. "The Web of Silence: Storytelling's Power to Hypnotize." *The National Storytelling Journal* 5 no. 2 (Spring/Summer 1988). Available on-line at: www.healingstory.org/articles/articles.html (6 June 2002).

Stone, Richard. The Healing Art of Storytelling: A Sacred Journey of Personal Discovery. New York: Hyperion, 1996.

Stossel, Scott. "The Man Who Counts the Killings," *Atlantic Monthly* 279 no. 5 (May 1997), 86-104.

Toffler, Alvin. *Future Shock.* New York: Harcourt Brace, 1970.

Trelease, Jim. *The Read-Aloud Hand-book.* 4th ed. New York: Penguin, 2001 [1982].

Vardamon, George T., and Patricia B. Vardaman. *Communication in Modern Organizations.* Malabar, Fla.: Krieger, 1982.

Weiner, Edith, and Arnold Brown. *Insider's Guide to the Future.* New York: The Boardroom, 1997.

Wiener, Norbert. *The Human Use of Human Beings: Cybernetics and Society*. Cambridge, Mass.: The Riverside Press, 1950.

Wolff, Michael. *Burn Rate: How I Survived the Gold Rush Years on the Internet*. New York: Touchstone Books, 1999.

Wolff, Michael. "Got It?" *Forbes ASAP* 5 (2 October 2000), 37-38.

Zipes, Jack. Creative Storytelling: Building Community, Changing Lives. New York: Routledge, 1995.

About the Author

Dr. Spaulding (B.A. Willamette University; M.L.S. University of Pittsburgh; D.L.S. Columbia University) began her career as a children's librarian for the New York Public Library. She went on to become the assistant storytelling and group work specialist and then the Children's Materials specialist for the 81-branch system. Currently, she is associate professor of Library and Information Science at the Palmer School of Library and Information Science of Long Island University. She has been active professionally, serving as a councilor for the American Library Association, chairing both the Caldecott and Notable Books for Children Committees, and chairing the Committee on the Profession for the New York Library Association, in addition to serving many other local, national and international committees, advisory panels and juries. In terms of storytelling, Dr. Spaulding told for the New York Public Library in branch libraries and at such locations as the Heckscher Oval of the Library and Museum for the Performing Arts at Lincoln Center, the New York Historical Society, and the Hans Christian Anderson Statue in Central Park. More recently, she has lectured, served as advisor and told stories for schools, churches, museums and other organization, such as NASA's Teacher Training Institute in Langley, Virginia, the Museum of American Folk Art in New York, *The Rainbow Channel* of Cablevision, and the Morrison Planetarium of the California Academy of Sciences in San Francisco. She has another book with the Scarecrow Press, *The Page as Stageset: Storyboard Picture Books*, about the way picture books began incorporating elements of popular culture like the comic, and should be viewed as a form of theater.